Photograph courtesy of King's College, Cambridge

Rupert Brooke

William E. Laskowski

Jamestown College

Twayne Publishers • New York
Maxwell Macmillan Canada • Toronto
Maxwell Macmillan International • New York Oxford Singapore Sydney

Rupert Brooke
William E. Laskowski

Twayne Publishers   Maxwell Macmillan Canada, Inc.
Macmillan Publishing Company   1200 Eglinton Avenue East
866 Third Avenue   Suite 200
New York, New York 10022   Don Mills, Ontario M3C 3N1

Library of Congress Cataloging-in-Publication Data

Laskowski, William E.
    Rupert Brooke / William E. Laskowski
        p.   cm.—(Twayne's English authors series; TEAS 504)
    Includes bibliographical references and index.
    ISBN 0-8057-7025-9
    1. Brooke, Rupert, 1887–1915 2. Poets, English—20th century—Biography.
3. War poetry, English—History and criticism. I. Title. II. Series.
PR6003.R4Z685 1994
823'.912—dc20   93-40510
                                                                      CIP

The paper used in this publication meets the minimum requirements of American
National Standard for Information Sciences—Permanence of Paper for Printed Library
Materials, ANSI Z39.48-1984.™♾

10 9 8 7 6 5 4 3 2 1

Printed in the United States of America.

To Dina, Billy, and Danny
my family

Contents

Preface

Perhaps no other poet has so often been described as physically resembling the god of poetry, of being an Apollo, as Rupert Brooke was, and the names of other deities and heroes often creep into descriptions of him: "Adonis," "the young Hermes," "David," "a Norse myth in modern clothes." Even such writers as Leonard Woolf and D. H. Lawrence, who disagreed violently with Brooke's politics, could not help describing him with such images. In a famous anecdote, Henry James, on first seeing Brooke, asked if Brooke's work was any good. When told it was not, James reportedly said, "Thank goodness. If he looked like that and was a good poet too, I do not know what I should do."[1] Such hyperbolic descriptions of physical beauty could not help but produce a reaction, a countermyth that arose soon after Brooke's death, and stood in opposition to the myth of the sunny Apollo who declaimed his poetry on the lawn of several picturesque old houses on the outskirts of Cambridge. This image of the charming, youthful bard became inextricably linked with the Georgian genre of poetry produced during the legendary long Edwardian garden party preceding the Great War—the first war that was given global proportions and that would, according to the myths that arose about it, decimate an entire generation, first and chief among them the beautiful young poet whose heroic war verse had initiated many other youths into the struggle.

The reaction to Brooke's death was all the more intensified by its timing and the political use that was made of it. Even before he died, the dean of St. Paul's read one of Brooke's war sonnets during an Easter sermon, and the first lord of the admiralty, Winston Churchill, wrote Brooke's obituary in the *Times* in his most orotund and vatic style. Even as Brooke's poems remained immensely popular both during and after the war, some soldiers began to question their appeal and their apparent denial of the reality of modern mechanized warfare, particularly after the indescribable slaughter of battles like the Somme and Passchendale. Men who had at first fought with a high sense of idealism came to forget the impetus which had strengthened them at the war's beginning; a myth soon arose about the Old Men who led a whole generation to its doom for no worthwhile reason. The literary generation that grew up after the war came to view Brooke and his war poems with the same sense of distrust and disgust accorded to the war atrocity stories which had impelled so many to enlist initially, stories later viewed as entirely false and mendacious. Further, Brooke's work, as well as the entire body of prewar Georgian poetry, became lumped together with the products of the prettified, pallid Georgianism that developed after the war, and all of it was aesthetically dismissed in favor of modernist poetry, which itself was a result as well as a description of the historical and psychic chasm the war had created. Thus, when World War II began, few poets dared to celebrate its beginnings, even though its war aims were much more justifiable, particularly in hindsight. The only poets who shared in Brooke's desire for cleansing combat were the young radical poets, such as John Cornford, who wrote about the Spanish civil war.[2]

Ever since Brooke's death, a devoted group of his friends has attempted to shield his reputation. His literary patron, Sir Edward Marsh, wrote a *Memoir* accompanying the first collected edition of Brooke's poems, which many of those who knew Brooke well felt to be a travesty, not adequately representing the full range of Brooke's personality. Some 50 years after his death, a proper edition of Brooke's letters had not yet appeared, and the only biography was marred by inaccuracies and florid overwriting. In 1964 the authorized biography was published, and for the first time the distasteful elements of Brooke's personality only hinted at before were revealed: his anti-Semitism, his antifeminism, his breakdown after a seemingly innocuous reading party at the end of 1911, and his paranoid reaction to a large group of people who had formerly been his friends. When a heavily edited edition of Brooke's letters was finally published in 1968, these aspects were only intensified, and readers learned the letters' publication had been delayed for more than 10 years in order to further protect Brooke's reputation. In 1987, a book about Brooke and his circle of friends, Paul Delaney's *The Neo-Pagans,* brought to light some of the most noxious material deleted from Sir Geoffrey Keynes's edition of the letters, and the demolition of Brooke's personality was complete. Brooke's politics, his art, and his life, once all so celebrated, had been weighed in new balances and found wanting.

The Brooke mythos and the reaction to it have made it almost impossible to disentangle the writer, the work, and the reputation. He has been the subject—and object—of so many polemics that it can be argued that he has never really been analyzed in the context of his times, either historically or artistically. Although it has been only hinted at before, Brooke is much more of a transitional figure than he has been given credit for. He is usually seen as representing the played-out end of

a bankrupt poetic tradition and as a blissful, almost criminally unconscious shill for a murderous war. According to this view, only when his
generation died could the fresh and truthful voice of modernism emerge.
Yet during his life, many critics thought that Brooke was daringly avant-
garde in his choice of subject matter and diction; this was often blamed
on the "regrettable" influence of John Donne on his poetry. Brooke also
shared some of the same literary interests and tastes as an American poet
living in London one year younger than himself, T. S. Eliot, and some
aspects of their personalities were curiously congruent. The point man of
the modernist movement, Ezra Pound, called Brooke the best of the
younger English poets. But most of this has been forgotten or neglected
in the aftermath of the Somme and *The Waste Land,* echoes of which are
still reverberating today. This is not to say that had Brooke lived (speculations about which are a favorite sport among Brooke critics), he would
have been a modernist; indeed, it seems likely he would have led the last
redoubts of Georgian entrenchment against modernism, which included
some of the more critically acclaimed war poets, such as Siegfried
Sassoon and Robert Graves. But he would have understood Pound and
above all Eliot more than any other Georgian seems to; he might have
continued to broaden Marsh's tastes and concepts of propriety as well.
Just before his death Brooke revealed a capacity to change and grow—
above all, to grow up. The most inaccurate portrait of Brooke that exists
is the one depicting him as an overgrown public school cricketeer blithe-
ly going off to war: "It's all great fun" is the quote most widely held
against him. In reality, Brooke realized exactly what would probably
happen to him when his battalion landed on the beaches at Gallipoli,
and he argued for better reasons for fighting than merely ridding
English culture of pernicious influences or as a socially acceptable way of
committing suicide. The entire concept of patriotism has been gradually
eroded in the West during the twentieth century, beginning with the
seemingly pointless carnage of World War I, but Brooke's definition of
patriotism arises directly out of the mainstream of English culture. To
understand Brooke in his cultural and artistic context is the ultimate
purpose of this study: not to rescue him but to comprehend him.

I would like to thank Faber and Faber, Ltd. as publishers for permission
to quote from Geoffrey Keynes's editions of *The Poetical Works* of Rupert
Brooke and *The Letters of Rupert Brooke,* and from *Rupert Brooke: A
Biography* by Christopher Hassall. I would also like to thank the staff of
the Raugust Library of Jamestown College and its head librarian, Phyllis

Bratton, for helping me obtain the materials to write this book, particularly Beth Sorenson and Carla Godfrey of Interlibrary Loan. Two of the people I would most have liked to read this book died while I was working on it. From my father I learned about the quiet daily heroism of fighting in a war and, much later, of fighting cancer, and also the joy in a task accomplished to the best of my ability. From Gloria Fromm I learned more than I can ever say about studying and writing about literature. I can only hope this book is worthy of the confidence and love they both gave to me.

And, of course, my abiding thanks to my wife, Dina, and my sons, Billy and Danny, the latter of whom arrived as I was completing this book; for their patience, support, and love, I am truly grateful.

Chronology

1887   Rupert Chawner Brooke born 3 August at Rugby, the second of three sons.

1897   Enters Hillbrow prep school as a day pupil.

1901   Enters Rugby in his father's house, School Field.

1904   Meets St. John Lucas; wins honorable mention in school competition for "The Pyramids."

1905   Visits Italy for health reasons. "The Bastille" wins school poetry prize. Vetted for Apostles by Lytton Strachey. Wins first of several *Westminster Gazette* poetry competitions. Wins scholarship to King's College, Cambridge.

1906   Wins King's Medal for Prose at Rugby for essay on William III. Enters King's College; forms with Hugh Dalton a reading group, the Carbonari. Plays the Herald in the *Eumenides*.

1907   Elder brother, Richard, dies. Brooke becomes Fabian Associate. Meets Hilaire Belloc. With Justin Brooke, forms the Marlowe Dramatic Society (MDS) at Cambridge, and plays Mephostopilis in *Dr. Faustus*.

1908   Becomes member 247 of the Cambridge Conversazione Society, better know as the Apostles. Meets H. G. Wells, G. B. Shaw, and the Webbs. Signs the Basis and becomes a Fabian Member. Meets Noel Olivier. Stage-manages and plays the Attendant Spirit in the MDS production of *Comus*.

1909   Receives a second in classics tripos. Moves into the Orchard at Grantchester. Meets Henry James. Elected president of Cambridge University Fabian Society. Proposes Basel 1933 scheme. Wins Charles Oldham Shakespeare Prize for essay on Webster. Incident with Denham Russell-Smith.

1910   On William Parker Brooke's death, becomes temporary housemaster of School Field. Travels on a caravan tour xiv

CHRONOLOGY

through southwest England speaking in favor of the Webbs' *Minority Report of the Poor Law Commission.* Makes secret engagement with Noel Olivier. Wins Harness Essay Prize at Cambridge for essay "Puritanism in the English Drama up to 1642." Gives lecture on "Democracy and the Arts" to the Fabian Society.

1911   First trip to Germany. Moves into the Old Vicarage, Grantchester. *Poems* published. Finishes first version of dissertation, *John Webster and the Elizabethan Drama.* Crisis at Lulworth over Ka Cox and Henry Lamb.

1912   Recuperates from breakdown at Cannes. Goes to Germany with Ka Cox. Returns to England; fails to get fellowship at King's. Returns to Germany; writes "The Old Vicarage, Grantchester" and the play *Lithuania.* Returns to England, often staying with Edward Marsh in London; helps Marsh plan *Georgian Poetry.* Rewrites dissertation. Meets Cathleen Nesbitt.

1913   Wins Fellowship at King's. Wins *Poetry Review* prize for "Grantchester." Travels to the United States and Canada, writing articles for the *Westminster Gazette.* Travels on to Hawaii, Samoa, Fiji, and New Zealand.

1914   Sails to Tahiti. Returns to England and social scene around Edward Marsh. In September enlists in Royal Naval Division with Marsh's help. Witnesses fall of Antwerp. Writes war sonnets.

1915   Leaves for Gallipoli expedition. Becomes ill in Egypt; refuses staff appointment. Dean Inge preaches Easter sermon in St. Paul's on "The Soldier." Brooke dies 23 April, on ship, of blood poisoning; buried on the island of the Skyros in the Aegean. Obituary in the *Times* by Winston Churchill.

Chapter One

Rupert Brooke: His Life

Rugby

Many critics have noted that Rupert Brooke's divided personality was prefigured in his full name, which was derived from personages from the time of the English civil war: Rupert, from the Royalist prince, and Chawner, after an ancestor who was an alleged regicide and a probable Puritan. Those inclinations of his which may be called "Royalist"—his posturings, his infatuation with the quotidian objects George Orwell called "the surface of the earth"[1]—were constantly at war with his puritanical side—a deep mistrust of his own sexual identity and sexuality. In the end, his puritanical side won out. This dominating aspect of his personality was instilled by his mother, however much he resisted her in all other matters (when Lytton Strachey began calling Brooke the "Rajah," after the White Rajah, James Brooke of Sarawak, Brooke himself came up with the nickname of the "Ranee" for his mother). In a family album questionnaire, his mother wrote that she valued "Earnestness of purpose" in a man and "moral courage" in a woman; the young Brooke revealingly responded "Fidelity" and "Wit" to the same questions (Hassall, 33).

The chief shaping force behind Brooke's personality, however, was the peculiar domestic circumstances of his upbringing. His father, William Parker Brooke, was a headmaster at Rugby and decidedly the less forceful of his parents (he was derisively nicknamed "Tooler" by the students for his nervous habit of unconsciously rummaging through his pockets, a nickname Brooke must have been uncomfortably well aware of). After attending prep school at nearby Hillbrow in Rugby, Brooke became a pupil in his father's house. As his biographers have pointed out, the often psychologically damaging environment of the normal British public school education at the beginning of the twentieth century, in which a young boy was taken away from home into a sometimes indifferent and often hostile environment, might ironically have been beneficial for Brooke, who instead had to combine home life with public school life. One form his rebellion took against this divided environment was the beginning of what became a lifelong habit of ill health; at school he was particularly susceptible to bouts of conjunctivitis. While some of these attacks were undoubtedly psychologically manipulative, his general neurasthenia tends to obscure the fact that his immune system seems to have been inherently weak and was a significant factor contributing to his celebrated death in the Aegean.

As it was, Brooke had to lead a kind of double life at Rugby, acting one way with his parents and another with his classmates. This duplicity led to what some critics have called his roles as a "jester and poseur"[2] as well as a "mimic and . . . ventriloquist."[3] Brooke's resistance took the habitual form of being "all things to all men," as he later admitted to one of his closest friends, Geoffrey Keynes (Hassall, 113). Brooke's first major pose was that of decadence. This form of rebellion was calculated to offend both his middle-class classmates and more particularly his parents, as he adopted the creed of the writer Oscar Wilde, who wrote a play satirizing all forms of Victorian "earnestness of purpose." "It is my obvious duty to live the aesthetic life I preach, and break the laws I loathe," he declaimed to Keynes (Hassall, 83). And while Brooke's decadent period lasts roughly from 1904, when he met and became friends with St. John Lucas, an older writer, to 1907, when he became a Fabian Associate, he was apt to drop into the decadent stance in his letters as late as 1912, if his correspondent knew him from that initial period. This decadent pose was a reaction to both the late Victorian liberalism of his parents and the hearty athleticism expected at Rugby ever since the school gave its name to the unique type of football invented there.

While at Hillbrow and Rugby Brooke also began the practice of cultivating circles of friends who often did not know of each other's existence, a practice later leading to charges that he compartmentalized his life. At this stage of his life, there were the decadents, chiefly Lucas and Arthur Eckersley; what might be called "pre-Bloomsbury," particularly the brothers of more famous writers, Maynard's brother Geoffrey Keynes and Lytton's brother James Strachey, as well as Virginia Stephen (with whom he once played cricket); and men like Hugh Dalton and Dudley Ward, who went on to distinguished careers in government service. With each of these groups he emphasized various aspects of his personality, but it was chiefly the decadent pose that colored his both his communications of this period and more particularly his verse, which he had been writing fairly seriously since 1903.

While his private verse concentrated on decadent themes and language, Brooke was also trying to succeed publicly with his poetry, for however much he tried to rebel against his parents, he did not want to go too far. His school poems on set historic themes, "The Pyramids" and "The Bastille," were prizewinners, and in 1905 he began entering poetry contests in various newspapers, especially the *Westminster Gazette,* contests that required poems written to what many writers would consider fruitlessly artificial constraints. Brooke enjoyed competing in these, not only for the monetary prizes, which often were his only independent source of income, but for the technical challenges they presented; despite his Apollonian looks, he did not particularly rely on poetic inspiration. Many friends who saw him work noted and even joked about his craftsmanlike approach to verse writing. Frances Cornford remarked that Brooke made poetry "feel more like carpentering" (Hassall, 276). Even while he was posing, he wanted his parents' approval, but on his own terms.

Cambridge

Part of this approval involved his going on to King's College, Cambridge, where his father had been the first Fellow who had not previously gone to Eton. Although during his first year there Brooke attempted to maintain his decadent posture (his room was decorated with Beardsley paintings), such affectations were passé at King's by then. When Lytton Strachey had surreptitiously vetted Brooke for possible admission to the Apostles, the secret discussion group also known as the Conversazione Society, he complained about the influence that St. John Lucas and Eckersley wielded over Brooke. Since Brooke had moved spatially as well as psychologically onward from his decadent circle of friends at Rugby, he had to discover new interests, one of which centered on the Apostles. At this time, the Apostles were, one is tempted to say, at their height; they were at least at the point of greatest interest to students of twentieth-century literature. Their active membership included many of the chief male figures in what was to be called Bloomsbury: the Stracheys, the Keyneses, Leonard Woolf, Roger Fry, Desmond MacCarthy, and E. M. Forster. If they were apostles of anybody at any time, it was during this decade, and their leader was the philosopher G. E. Moore. As Paul Levy has shown, Brooke was almost immediately taken into the Moorean inner circle at the time, and invited on Moore's exclusive Easter reading trips[4] (an invitation never extended to, for instance, Bertrand Russell). Moore's philosophy, as chiefly stated in *Principia Ethica,* became extremely significant for Brooke (although much of it initially came through osmosis, for it appears he did not read the work until 1910), both in the uses he made of it in prose and verse and in his later reaction against it. The Apostles imparted to Brooke a facility in handling abstract concepts and ideas, a facility somewhat weakened by his characteristic tendency toward playfulness. They were also a group he could not mention to his parents, because of its secret nature and its strongly homosexual atmosphere at the time, an atmosphere against which Brooke was later to violently rebel.

Politics grew into another major interest in Brooke's life at this time. His parents (especially his mother) were staunch Liberals, and while at school at Rugby Brooke had campaigned hard for a Liberal candidate. He also admitted that he posed as a socialist at Rugby to pique his middle-class classmates, who looked on socialists "as demons only one degree in the ranks of the Pit less wicked than Artists."[5] At Cambridge Brooke became acquainted with the Fabian Society, the socialist gradualists led at this time by Beatrice and Sydney Webb, G. B. Shaw, and H. G. Wells, all of whom he met at Cambridge. While Brooke was initially impressed by reading *News from Nowhere* to the point of declaring that he was a follower of William Morris, the Fabian pamphlets, full of statistics and facts, and the works and personal influence of Wells led him to sign the Fabian Basis and join the Fabian Society. Temperamentally, Brooke seemed to some to have been unsuited to becoming a Fabian (he never personally impressed Beatrice Webb), and some of his nonchalant posturing in his letters—"acting on one's Conscience is always rather fun," he wrote of attending the Fabian summer school (*L,* 255)—have led later critics to doubt his commitment. Brooke was, however, as devoted to the Fabians as he was to any cause in his life: during the summer of 1910 he studied facts and statistics diligently and then, accompanied by Hugh Dalton, traveled by caravan through the south of England speaking in favor of the Webbs' proposal to reform the English poor laws. But there was always an element of *épater le bourgeois* in his socialism; for instance, when he met the premier of Canada on his travels there, he wrote a note with the letter of introduction declaiming, "I am an English Socialist and a writer" (Hassall, 405), a political declaration that nevertheless did not carry over very much into the journalism he was writing about his travels.

Brooke's other main interest at Cambridge was drama. His first role was a minor one, the Herald in the *Eumenides,* but his striking looks impressed themselves on members of the audience, most importantly Edward Marsh, who perhaps played the most significant role in

Brooke's life outside of his mother. The Amateur Dramatic Society at Cambridge at this time concentrated on lighter works, especially comedies. Brooke and many of his friends (most importantly Justin Brooke, no relation) shared in the growing resurgence of interest at this time in Elizabethan literature and drama, and they formed the Marlowe Dramatic Society, whose first production, naturally enough, was *Dr. Faustus,* in which Brooke played Mephostopilis, to mixed reviews (he seems to have deliberately hidden his looks, and his acting of verse was never, according to witnesses, as effective as his reading of poetry to friends). The last major production that Brooke was involved in was a three-hundredth anniversary production of *Comus,* which he stage-managed and in which he played the role of the Attendant Spirit. The subject of Milton's masque, chastity, would loom large in Brooke's psychological development. Brooke's theatrical experiences led him to declare later, when depressed about his verse writing, that he wanted to become a theater manager and playwright; however, he never seriously pursued the position.

In all these activities, Brooke's circle of friends and acquaintances widened, and for the only time in his life, overlapped. Most of them formed a group Virginia Woolf came to call the "Neo-pagans," many of whom had attended Bedales, a progressive coeducational public school founded near the end of the nineteenth century. These friends included Jacques Raverat, a Frenchman sent to school in England, and the four attractive daughters of the Fabian diplomat Sydney Olivier. There were also the younger generation of the Cambridge intellectual aristocracy, including Gwen Darwin (who later married Raverat) and Frances Darwin (who married Francis Cornford), as well as Katherine (universally called "Ka") Cox, a student at Newnham College who was active in the Fabians and dramatics. As Paul Delaney has shown, this group was a somewhat unsuccessful attempt to rebel against the Victorian proprieties that to a great extent still governed relationships between young men and women in Edwardian England. Their beliefs and practices, which centered on unchaperoned outings, often in natural settings, grew out of the "simple life" and back-to-nature movements of Edward Carpenter and others (which led to the neo-pagans' sarcastic nickname of "dew-dabblers"); however, while they believed in a greater intimacy between the sexes, it did not extend to physical intimacy, and gave rise to the confusion Beatrice Webb noted in Fabian sexual mores: "we none of us know what exactly is the sexual code we believe in—approving of many things on paper which we violently object to when they are practised by those we care about."[6] In Brooke's case, this uncertainty contributed heavily to his nervous breakdown in early 1912.

Vocation

Brooke's range of interests at Cambridge caused him to spread himself too thin, a danger his tutor had in mind when advising Brooke against his accepting the editorship of the *Cambridge Review*. In addition to the Apostles, Brooke formed and led another discussion group, the Carbonari, with Hugh Dalton, and he was president of the Marlowe Dramatic Society and the Cambridge chapter of the Fabian Society. Also, while he concentrated on classics (a fact he never let his unclassical friends forget about when he wrote them), he never seemed too interested in the subject, and his majoring in it was more out of filial duty than inclination. He was noticeably indolent before his exams, and when he received a disappointing second in his classics tripos (a grade that may have been overgenerous for his performance), he was chiefly worried about the effect the results would have on his parents. His main problem was that he lacked a real vocation. He wrote verse, but much of what had been published was made to order, and obviously minor. His interest in politics led to no political ambitions. The only opening left was the profession of his immediate family, academics (his uncle was dean of King's), and since a specialization in classics was debarred by his poor performance, he began to concentrate on English literature, particularly the plays of John Webster and other Elizabethan dramatists. His official ambition was thus to become a don. He therefore moved into the first of his "rural" retreats, a picturesque house named the Orchard in Grantchester, ostensibly to concentrate on his thesis, but in reality to socialize and skinny-dip with friends and acquaintances, and here he began to forge the main basis for his legend. Its origins are implicit in the photographs of the barefoot, open-shirted poet reciting his verses to an enchanted circle of like-minded young friends, in the neo-pagan version of what has become more widely perceived to be an endless garden party in a golden Edwardian summer.

Part of Brooke's reluctance to settle on a career was caused by what must be bluntly called his simple reluctance to grow up, what Geoffrey Keynes has dryly termed his "rather slow achievement of a completely adult mentality" (*L*, xii). Brooke had a real and abiding fear of maturity. Part of this fear may have been generational. He once remarked that

"Nobody over thirty is worth talking to" (Hassall, 108) (an attitude that was to come into greater vogue some 50 years later). Significantly, even though he later admitted that James Barrie was a sentimentalist, one of his favorite plays was *Peter Pan*. "It was perfect," he wrote to Keynes. "It is merely & completely the incarnation of all one's childish dreams—the best dreams, almost, that one has" (*L*, 19). And while the convention of calling one's correspondent "child" may have been widespread at the time, no one used it more relentlessly in his letters than Brooke did, especially with women.

Brooke's love of "Never Land" led to his devising, with Bryn and Margery Olivier and Dudley Ward, what he called in a key letter to Raverat "The SCHEME," or "the Organized Chance of Living Again" (*L*, 195). In 1933, a group of friends would, to use a phrase from a generation Brooke would have felt quite at home in, "drop out" of their jobs and ordinary lives and meet each other at the train station in Basel, Switzerland. They feared turning into what Brooke called, using another habitual image, "fat, dead, top-hatted, ghosts, haunting the civilization that was their ruin" (*L*, 193). He foresaw himself turning into a middle-aged, suburban "literary hack" whose escape would be viewed as a suicide (a fate he elsewhere jokingly predicted would happen to the Apostles in the 1920s). What they would do after they met was immaterial; they would "be *living* . . . glorious at fifty! . . . children seventy-years, instead of seven" (*L*, 194–95). Brooke, who for much of his life and in much of his verse searched for a replacement for the Christian afterlife he no longer believed in, declared that "there's a better Heaven than the pale serene Anglican windless harmonium-buzzing Eternity of the Christians, a Heaven in Time, now and for ever, ending for each, staying for all, a Heaven of Laughter and Bodies and Flowers and Love and People and Sun and Wind, in the only place we know or care for, ON EARTH" (*L*, 195). Many critics have pointed out the melancholy reality of this group's actual situation in 1933: Brooke and Raverat dead, Bryn Olivier sick with the aplastic anemia that was to kill her two years later, Margery Olivier institutionalized with schizophrenia, and across the Swiss border, Adolf Hitler coming into power. Yet because of these characteristic themes—ghosts, children, and heaven—this letter is not so much a "Neo-pagan manifesto," as Paul Delaney has called it (Delaney, 72), but more a précis of Brooke's personal credo—an avoidance of reality, adulthood, responsibility, and parenthood: in his own words, "the escape back into youth" (*L*, 194).

Brooke in Love

Some three weeks after this letter to Raverat, Brooke was thanking a 16-year-old young woman for pointing out "the danger of" the scheme "degenerating into a tourist fortnight upon the Continent."[7] This young woman, Noel Olivier, would continue to offer Brooke such sensible, sound advice, often much to his chagrin, because almost immediately after they first met at a dinner at Cambridge for her father, Brooke realized he was attracted to her, and in a pattern that was characteristic of many of his relationships, he began to idolize her. She became the first romantic interest in his life, and it is almost fair to use a cliché and say that he never got over her. The main obstacle to their establishing a relationship was her age; even though the neo-pagans considered themselves enlightened beyond their Victorian predecessors, this did not extend to interfering with a young woman's education and social development. While Noel was not the only Olivier sister Brooke was romantically interested in, she quickly became his focus, and her older sisters, who often had to act in loco parentis while their parents were in Jamaica, tried to slow the pace of Brooke's involvement. Much of Brooke's correspondence as this time involves setting up surreptitious "coincidental" meetings with Noel Olivier, to the extent of visiting Edward Thomas at Bedales to see her and poring over train timetables so that rendezvous could be arranged at line crossings.

At first Noel Olivier was flattered by Brooke's attention, but unwilling to become more deeply involved with him. In many ways her personality was the antithesis of Brooke's: level-headed, commonsensical, and objective. Eventually, however, she could not resist the appeals of someone whom Yeats called "the handsomest man in England" (Hassall, 374), and on a summer outing in 1910 she agreed to become secretly engaged to him. It was a decision she almost immediately came to regret. She realized she was not in love with him; at first she blamed it on "this beastly indifference in me" (SOL, 74). She later explained—in the third person, ever mindful of Brooke's tendency to react violently to rejection—that he was "very beautiful, everyone who sees him loves him. . . . I fell in love with him, as I had fallen in love with other people before, only this time it seemed final—as it had, indeed, every time. . . . Since then I have gradually begun to know him better, & would I think, have looked on him as a friend. . . . [H]e & history made me believe that I was a lover as well as he. I'm not, Rupert. I'm affectionate, reverent, anything you like but not that" (*SOL*, 81–82). Brooke found it impossible to believe in or to accept her rejection, even this delicately phrased.

What Noel Olivier hinted at in this letter—that her rejection of Brooke was caused by elements in his personality that he had unwittingly revealed to her—was becoming more and more evident during this period. Contributing to his stress over his career was his father's death in 1910 after a short illness, an event that was mentally painful to his family. As he wrote to Dudley Ward, "we all talked of other things and Mother and I kept looking at Father, and at each other, and nobody dared to say the things they thought, and there were words floating in the air and in the brain and in the middle of conversation one suddenly saw them and felt unable to speak" (*L*, 211). The lack of emotional posturing in this brief statement is uncharacteristic and significant; Brooke was much more emotionally upset over his father's death than he otherwise let on. Much later, at one of the last times he saw Noel Olivier, he was able to control his feelings, and he proudly told Raverat, "Haven't felt so pleased with myself since Father died" (*SOL*, 273). Brooke was always proud when he proved to himself that he could control his emotions. Part of his emotional anxiety at this time was caused by the financial circumstances into which his father's death placed his family; he was forced temporarily to take his father's place as housemaster of School Field only five years after he had attended it. While he referred to this experience as housemaster sarcastically to friends, it must have been stressful. His years at Rugby, particularly after he had gone up to Cambridge, he had remembered as idyllic: "As I looked back at five years I seemed to see almost every hour golden and radiant and always increasing in beauty as I grew more conscious, and I could not (and cannot) hope for or ever quite imagine such happiness elsewhere" (Hassall, 142). The tone of this remembrance may have been another pose, but as many of Brooke's biographers have noted, his first year at Cambridge was upsetting to him because his position there represented a demotion from the position he had held at Rugby. To be reminded of this at a point in his life when he was trying to establish his permanent role was unsettling.

Another element in Brooke's life about which he could not make up his mind concerned his sexuality. At Rugby he had entered into several mildly homoerotic "crushes," and at Cambridge much of this atmosphere persisted in the group surrounding the Apostles; however, the more blatant overtures of the latter Brooke seems to have found upset-

ting. Yet in 1909 he did experiment with homosexuality one night with
Denham Russell-Smith, an incident he later wrote about in explicit
detail in a letter to James Strachey (perhaps to confound him, because of
Strachey's frequent though unsuccessful sexual advances toward
Brooke).[8] This seems to have been the only time he overtly referred to
the incident, although he hinted that he was thinking about such matters in a letter to his cousin, Erica Cotterill, a few months before (*L*,
173). The letter to Strachey was not, of course, included in Keynes's official edition of the *Letters*. This incident seems to have arisen because
Brooke wanted to lose what he called his "chastity"; he also wanted to
discover his own sexual identity. Brooke was well aware of his looks,
which even Leonard Woolf, who otherwise seems to have been immune
to Brooke's charms, called "stunning—it is the only appropriate adjective."[9] And there was a feminine aspect to his appeal; time and again, his
complexion and facial coloring are described as girlish—"the look of a
great girl," in Edward Thomas's memorable phrase (Hassall, 240).
Brooke must have been aware of this as well; he disgustedly reports in a
letter an older woman's compliment to his mother, "He has a skin like a
girl's—He looks very like a girl" (*L*, 348). Part of Brooke's later violent
paranoia about Bloomsbury was based in his reaction against this widespread perception of himself physically by others, and perhaps even by
himself.

As Noel Olivier gradually tried to temper Brooke's ardor, he found
himself increasingly attracted to Ka Cox during the year 1911. Cox was
the mother figure in the neo-pagan circle, a role she learned in raising
her younger sisters after their mother died (she later nursed Virginia
Woolf through one of her breakdowns). In many of his relationships
(including that with Cathleen Nesbitt), Brooke was searching for some
kind of maternal warmth: "I've that long-ago feeling of a 'lap,' a place
you hid your face in, and shelved responsibilities," he wrote to Cox (*L*,
354). She appears to have been relatively unprepossessing physically (a
fact some of Brooke's biographers have not phrased quite so delicately),
but she attracted a fair number of suitors. Her relationship with Brooke
appears to have heated up early in 1911, especially at an incident in a
bookshop during which Brooke appears to have been insensitive. His
overreaction to whatever did happen is striking in its language: "I'm red
and sick with anger at myself for my devilry and degradation and stupidity. . . . But I hurt you, I hurt you, Ka, for a bit, unforgiveably and
filthily and infamously" (*L*, 269); the overtones of sexual guilt in the
nouns and adverbs hint at the underlying nature of Brooke's breakdown

a year later. As one reads between the lines of Brooke's correspondence with Cox during 1911, it becomes clear that Brooke's frustration with Noel Olivier's resistance, coupled with his own sexual needs, the nature of which became clearer to him after his encounter with Russell-Smith, had led him to concentrate on Cox as the object of his sexual attentions. In that first overapologetic letter he declares that he "couldn't, as I wanted, take hold of you and put mouth hard to mouth, for you had somehow put that aside, and it would have confused other issues, and— I daredn't" (*L,* 269). Later on that year Cox hinted to Brooke that others might think she and Brooke had some kind of exclusive relationship, and when she asked Brooke if Geoffrey Keynes might have a picture of her painted by Duncan Grant, Brooke angrily replied, "We don't copulate without marriage, but we do meet in cafes, talk on buses, go on unchaperoned walks, stay with each other, give each other books, without marriage" (*L,* 304), so he didn't understand what his problem really involved. Later, however, he indicated that he was thinking about physical matters: "and the bed's so comfortable (and so big . . . I beg pardon). . . . You're so fine. But I'll wake you up a lot yet. And I'll tell you all the secrets of Hell: and you shall tell me unmentionable things" (*L,* 320). However much their group might be "awfully honest and genteel and chaste and self-controlled and nice" (*L,* 304), Brooke, with these insinuations that he was thinking about a physical relationship with Cox, revealed that he was getting ready for, in Delaney's words, "radically changing the game as it had been played up to now" among their circle (Delaney, 139).

During this period Brooke was under the pressure of preparing two of his major works: his dissertation on John Webster, which required two versions, and *Poems* (1911), the only volume of his poetry published during his lifetime. For the dissertation he had to read a great number of Elizabethan and Jacobean plays, an experience that in itself he found almost restful: "Reading and reading and reading. It's not noble, but it's so happy" (*L,* 311). One reason he was so happy was his move from The Orchard to the building he would make so famous—or notorious—a year later in a poem initially entitled "Home": the Old Vicarage in Grantchester. The writing of the dissertation, often in London, later that year was less idyllic. Seeing his volume of poems through the press was also troubling. He had disagreements with Frank Sidgwick over the propriety of several of what have been called his "unpleasant" or "ugly" poems, particularly "Lust" and "A Channel Passage." He was forced to give in over "Lust," retitling it "Libido," a concession which he stub-

bornly corrected by hand in copies he sent to friends. The other problem
with publishing his poems was that he had changed as a poet and to a
certain extent no longer believed in what he had written during his
decadent period. While he wrote to Edward Marsh about "the promising
verses of a young poet, called Rupert Brooke, who died in 1908" (*L,*
327), perhaps because he realized Marsh would appreciate that type of
verse more, he was more revelatory to Sybil Pye; he told her that he
liked the current poems "by *me,* not by a frail pleasant youth of the same
name who died in 1908" (*L,* 326). His abandonment of his previous
poetic persona was the argument he pursued with Sigdwick in urging
the inclusion of more "realistic" poems; much of his other verse con-
tained "unimportant prettiness. There's plenty of that sort of wash in the
other pages for the readers who like it" (*L,* 315–16). Thus, Brooke found
himself at this point trying to establish both his professional and poetic
identity and, more important psychologically, his sexual identity.

Lulworth

All these factors contributed to what has become known as the Lulworth
incident—Brooke's confrontation with Bloomsbury over Ka Cox—
which led to a prolonged nervous breakdown, Brooke's physical affair
with Cox, a fundamental change in many of his attitudes, and an exacer-
bation of several of his most repellent tendencies. It was certainly the
most crucial event in Brooke's life, so important that John Lehmann
begins his study of Brooke with an account of it. As many commentators
have pointed out, the precise details of what happened at Lulworth will
probably never be known, but what has been insufficiently emphasized
is that the psychological pressure that culminated in Lulworth had been
building up for more than a year; adding to the pressure was that just
before Lulworth, on 15 December, as Pippa Harris has revealed, Brooke
had decided to break with Noel Olivier, announcing "he could not continue their relationship, until Noel was prepared to make more of a commitment" (*SOL,* 144 n. 1). His letters to her in the period just before this
declaration indicate his instability and mounting hysteria; at the end of
November he wrote, "If you take the least notice of my silliness, I'll kill
you. If you don't, I'll kill myself. Forgive! At least I dare take off all my
clothes before you!" (*SOL,* 139).

Another underemphasized contributing factor to the Lulworth crisis
is the manic-depressive element in Brooke's personality. He reveals this
aspect directly in several letters written in the year preceding the inci-

dent. "Did you ever feel, when you were a child, about once every six months, a sudden waking, and a knowledge that you were, somehow, on a higher level, & that all the rest of the time you'd been thinking you were living, but really asleep?" he wrote to Keynes. "There were two grades of life, A & B, and the A periods signalled to each other across the valleys. But it was only in A you really knew the difference" (*L*, 292). He admitted that he felt this way again now in Munich, on a manic upswing. And to Frances Cornford he wrote in his faux wistful vein at the same time, "Dear! dear! it's very trying being ever so exalted one day & ever so desperate the next—this self-knowledge" (*L*, 279). In his euphoric states he would exclaim to his correspondent, usually a woman in whom he was romantically interested at the time, that, inspired by her, he could do anything. For example, to Cathleen Nesbitt he later declared, "I want to walk a thousand miles, and write a thousand plays, and sing a thousand poems, and drink a thousand pots of beer, and kiss a thousand girls" (*L*, 437); several weeks later he became more specific: "I want to write ten pages to you: to finish a play of Tchekoff's: to write several poems: to start a play I've thought of: right through the night: tasting it all: anything so long as I'm *working* at it. And at dawn to run three miles and bathe" (*L*, 453). These feverish promises seldom amounted to much; revealingly, the only play he ever completed, *Lithuania,* was rarely alluded to in his letters while he was writing it. On the other end of the emotional spectrum, Brooke, when subjected to great stress, whether from jealousy or loneliness, was apt to fall into a severe depression, the most serious of which occurred at Lulworth.

The bare bones of what happened there are that Brooke had organized a reading party of friends, including Ka Cox, during the Christmas holidays at Lulworth at the end of 1911. Lytton Strachey brought down the painter Henry Lamb to join them, and at one point during the holiday Cox informed Brooke that she was in love with Lamb. Brooke reacted violently against this: he became intensely jealous of Lamb and was convinced Lytton Strachey had acted as "pimp" in bringing Cox and Lamb together. He almost immediately lapsed into what biographers have called a nervous breakdown and what he later termed "a foodless & sleepless hell" (*L*, 359). Therapy for this condition at the time consisted of complete rest and overeating, which Brooke proceeded to undergo at Cannes with his mother. While there he surreptitiously wrote to Cox to arrange a meeting with her later in Europe. These letters are among the most unpleasant things Brooke ever wrote; in them all his neuroses are revealed: "Oh, it's all mixed up with this chastity, and everything's a whirl, and still I'm mad and tiny and frightened" (*L,* 335). His sexual jealousy of Lamb exacerbated his own physical attraction to Cox, which he had hinted at to her but controlled throughout the previous year. When he told her in a letter from Cannes of his thoughts during an evening they'd spent together two years earlier—that he had "looked at the firm and lovely place where your deep breasts divided and grew out the chest and went down under the dress" (*L,* 344)—it is obvious what kind of relationship he wished to establish with her. He also, however, couched his desires in more characteristic images: "But I'm certainer than ever that I'm, possibly, opening new Heavens, like a boy sliding open the door into a big room; trembling between wonder and uncertainty" (*L,* 335). Simultaneously mixed up with this sexual longing are phrases indicating that the puritan elements of his nature were not far from the surface: "I'm ingratitude dirty, dirty, dirty" (*L,* 336). However much he tried to balance these attitudes within himself—"And I think of your gentle strong soft body—my thoughts are entirely indecent and entirely clean" (*L,* 355)—such a psychic reconciliation was to be only temporary.

Cox was eventually able to join Brooke, and they spent some time together in Germany living as man and wife. The code of conduct of their circle, however, demanded honesty, and she admitted to Brooke that she had seen Lamb again in London, a declaration that catapulted Brooke into another breakdown, which caused them to return to England. This is the most obscure section of the whole affair. Something occurred for which Brooke would never forgive Cox, and from all accounts it was merely this admission of seeing Lamb again, unless this revelation was accompanied by a declaration that all the while she loved Lamb, and only gave in to Brooke's pleadings out of sympathy. Nevertheless, the intensity and durability of Brooke's reaction are remarkable. He later declared to Noel Olivier, "Ka's done the most evil things in the world. She has—or she's on the way to have—dirtied good & honour & all high things, & betrayed & degraded love. Think of the filthiest image you can for the fouling of the best things by the worst. Ka is doing that. . . . I'd not care if I saw Ka *dying* of some torture I could inflict on her, slowly" (*SOL,* 168). After statements like this, one can easily see why Noel Olivier quickly retreated from further intimacy with Brooke.

After his father died, Brooke, musing about his parents' influence on his personality, told E. J. Dent, "But I've always felt so especially unlike and separate from my parents—in good and bad qualities alike—I'm wholly an individualist" (*L*, 220). Yet never was he blinder, than when he did not see how much his mother's rigid sexual morality was mirrored in his own. Paradoxically, throughout his critical writings Brooke excoriated the Puritans and their moral code. In his prize-winning essay on William III written at Rugby, he accused that monarch of possessing "the intolerable gloom of Puritanism" (Hassall, 91). Significantly, the subject of his later prize-winning essay at Cambridge was "Puritanism in the English Drama up to 1642." In it he criticized the Puritans for exhibiting many of the same faults he was so troubled with at this time: "for by the insidious dualism which lay, psychologically as theologically behind Puritanism—that which was not of the soul was material and dangerous."[10] Brooke elsewhere claimed that his circle's ethos was able to reconcile the sensual and the ascetic, using ideas and language from E. M. Forster's latest novel, *Howards End*: "The Puritans dimly try to build up the background: the hedonist flaps inconsistently for the thing. *We* go for both; we join up Puritan and Hedonist: we have (once more) only connected" (*L*, 302). Nonetheless, even his closest friends noted that he seemed emotionally drawn to these religious zealots who intellectually repelled him; as Frances Cornford, perhaps his most perceptive friend, remembers, "Deep-ingrained in him, and handed down to him I should imagine through generations of English ancestors, was the puritanical spirit. I remember how clearly it showed when he spoke the Chorus in Faustus in some sort of Puritan scholar's dress. And nobody could miss it, whoever saw the scorn and sternness in his face when he spoke of things that he hated, things corrupt and unclean" (Hassall, 277–78). Subsequently Brooke would adapt what he considered an equally distinguishing Puritan characteristic—their English patriotism—to his own personality just before the start of the war.

What happened next to Brooke and Cox would have been ironic were it not so pitiable. To put it simply, Cox fell in love with Brooke while he plummeted out of love with her. They returned to Germany, but both were ill, so they returned to England, and Brooke was soon telling friends that he was now emotionally numb, with one important exception: "I've no feeling for anybody at all—except the uneasy ghosts of the immense reverence and rather steadfast love for Noel and a knowledge that Noel is the finest thing I've ever seen in the world, and Ka—isn't" (*L*, 378). Once Cox had removed her own inaccessibility, Brooke found himself inevitably turning back to another inaccessible object. Cox, however, was now in love with Brooke and thought they would eventually get married. Further complicating matters was that Cox apparently became pregnant, and while most biographers (based on Cathleen Nesbitt's account) mention that the child was stillborn, one unsubstantiated report claims she had an abortion. Cox was devastated at the turn Brooke's emotions had taken; as she said later, "You don't know how awful it is when one has broken down that wall of separation that one lives in and let another human being come right in, to have to live alone again" (Hassall, 351). She never got over her relationship with Brooke. Virginia Woolf complained about Cox in 1927, "Why can't she ever wake up from the year 1911? There she sticks with Rupert copulating in Berlin and Dudley Ward and Gwen and Jacques. Pah!"[11] All of this might have been ironic in a rather macabre fashion had Brooke not revealed himself to be such a thoroughly unsympathetic character throughout the whole imbroglio: "The bother is I don't really like [Cox], at all. There is a feeling of staleness, ugliness, trustlessness about her. I don't know. Dirt.—hu— . . . I've sort of a hunger for cleanness" (*L*, 379).

One consequence of this "cleanness" in Brooke's mind involved what many readers today would find the most offensive aspect of Brooke's personality: his anti-Semitism. As has been pointed out, it was almost naive of Brooke's friends to suppress the more explicit sexual portions of Brooke's correspondence and biography in the interests of safeguarding his image, while allowing many of the anti-Semitic remarks to remain. Brooke's protectors attempt to exculpate his anti-Semitism in a variety of ways: that Brooke's prejudices were of his time; that he had been infected by reading Hilaire Belloc; that the Lulworth episode inflamed a mild propensity into a phobia; and that he indulged himself only with like-minded friends such as the Raverats, who had become somewhat militant Christians. All of these excuses, while true to a certain extent, do not bear close scrutiny. While many other writers of Brooke's generation (indeed, too many before the Holocaust) do exhibit anti-Semitic attitudes, few outside of Ezra Pound share Brooke's zeal: "Why is it you can almost *see* a Jew's tail go between his legs?" he once wrote (*L*, 298). Although Belloc was a notorious anti-Semite, Brooke does not seem to have been influenced very much by the theoretical component of Belloc's anti-Semitism, which had its origins in William Cobbett's economic theories in the early nineteenth century. For instance, Brooke's favorite work by Belloc was *The Four Men,* which is full of veiled allusions to "moneylenders" and "usurers," terminology Brooke seemed utterly uninterested in. (Brooke, however, like G. K. Chesterton and Belloc, was incensed by the Marconi scandal and Rufus Isaacs's role in it.) Brooke's anti-Semitism predated the Lulworth crisis, and correspondents with whom he shared anti-Semitic remarks include his mother, E. J. Dent, Edward Marsh, and Lady Eileen Wellesley, as well as the Raverats.

Another group that, according to Brooke's unbalanced mind, was spreading a malignant moral infection was Bloomsbury. Brooke's relationship with its members had always been somewhat wary, since many of them, including Leonard Woolf, E. M. Forster, and Lytton Strachey, felt he was too much the self-conscious charmer with a correspondingly hard inside, while he never felt absolutely comfortable in their homosexual atmosphere. As Paul Levy has noted, Brooke was "not so easy-going" as other Apostles about joking concerning "the Higher Sodomy," and he revealed his attitude to them in a 1909 Apostles paper, "Why Not Try the Other Leg?" (Levy, 261). Pressures had also been building up in the year before Lulworth when Bloomsbury indulged in another of its favorite practices—gossiping—about Brooke and Cox. He complained to her: "Ka, they've been Talking, about You and Me. Talking! Awful. If you only knew what James said Virginia said So and So said. . . . All the worst things drive them on. The furtive craving to interfere in other people's lusts, the fear of unusual events, and the rest. The mother and the clergyman are at one in these kind hearts. False ethics and funk have Raised one another. They live for the future like Puritans and judge by the end like Parsons" (*L,* 313). At Lulworth these pressures imploded, and Brooke saw Lytton Strachey as the chief culprit behind Cox's possible (or actual) seduction by Lamb, although Strachey later seems to have worked harder to thrust Brooke and Cox together. (Ironically, Strachey's biographer, Michael Holroyd, finds that Brooke's "epistolary style . . . bears many similarities to Lytton's own.")[12] Brooke never forgave Lytton Strachey for this imagined betrayal, and he soon saw a moral conspiracy spread throughout the entire Bloomsbury group. He grew cold toward one of his oldest friends, James Strachey, who, when a witness of Brooke's refusal to shake his brother's hand in public, termed Brooke's mental condition "paranoia," an obsession Brooke would later display even in the war sonnets. While Brooke seemed to remain warmest toward Virginia Woolf of all the Bloomsbury set, he never forgot that Leonard Woolf was Jewish. Although he later told Raverat that he found Bloomsbury to be "people I find pleasant and remarkable as individuals," he worried about women he had idealized, such as Noel Olivier, being tainted by "the subtle degradation of the collective atmosphere" there (*L,* 380). After reading the available correspondence, however, one has to ask, in what way was Brooke better for Cox than Henry Lamb would have been? To his credit, near the end of his life Brooke asked

himself the same question and came up with the painfully obvious
answer: his own effect on Cox's life had been ruinous.

Brooke's faint hopes for a reconciliation with Noel Olivier were
doomed by his relentless honesty to her about Cox, an obsessive open-
ness that revealed his mind to be in a seriously disturbed state and was
to become all too evident in his resumed communications with Olivier.
When he learned she would go camping with James Strachey but not
with him, he used emotional blackmail to get her to see him again: "Or,
of course, I might just be driven more desperate than ever. . . . You may
have persuaded yourself you don't love me. . . . And, by God, if I do kill
myself, I'd like to do it with one fairly decent memory behind" (SOL,
218–19). And while he could lightheartedly tell Cathleen Nesbitt, an
attractive young actress, that he would kidnap her and take her to his
own version of a bower of bliss, his speculations about kidnapping to
Olivier are more disturbing and again drift off into a fantasy in which
his death would punish her: "So many people get kidnapped nowadays:
& you're always drifting about alone. Please. I'm perfectly serious—be
careful. When I lie awake at nights—Don't ever, on any pretext, go off
with people you don't know, however well authenticated, or get into
cabs—it's impossible to be too careful. I demand this. . . . What I hope
is that, at some crossing, when you're just going to be run over by a
motor-bus, one of these days, I may pull you out of the way, & get run
over myself. It'd be a good way out of a bloody world for me: & I
should go with the satisfaction of knowing that you'd feel horribly
awkward for a great many weeks, or months" (SOL, 231). When dis-
secting their relationship later, she more bluntly told him, "It was your
particularly unpleasant sense of humour which finally killed me off, of
course" (SOL, 250). Brooke's humor, in the indulgence of which he
always had a tendency to step beyond the bounds of his correspondent's
propriety, was never more prone to veering off into hysteria and self-
pity than at this time.

Recovery

When Brooke found himself in Germany after breaking up with Cox, he
used his perhaps most characteristic image to refer to the manner in
which he thought he could heal himself. He wrote to Keynes, "shall we
bathe? I haven't bathed since November. There's a lot to wash off. . . . It
may be there is a herb growing at the bottom of the river just above the
pool at Grantchester, & that if I dive & find it & bring it up—it will heal

me" (*L,* 389). About three weeks later in July, he wrote to Noel Olivier about the results, "And now I'm this—July & December *don't* really link up. There's a discontinuity. . . . I've bathed. It seemed to wash off a good deal" (*SOL,* 190–91). Brooke's predilection for nude bathing, particularly with members of the opposite sex, was well known; since to a certain degree it was an outgrowth of the Bedalian progressive educational philosophy, it was almost entirely innocent, and Brooke's cobathers included the Olivier sisters, Virginia Stephen (later Woolf), and almost certainly the novelist Rose Macaulay. To Brooke this type of bathing was almost sacramental—it held for him the promise of washing away not so much his sins as his self-conscious awareness of his body, and the deeper he plunged into that element, the more assured he felt of restoration and redemption. This particular type of secular baptism was one of his most durable images, making its last and to some critics most disturbing appearance in the first of the war sonnets, "Peace."

While alone in Germany, Brooke, despite his psychic condition, produced two of his most sustained works: "The Old Vicarage, Grantchester," and the one-act drama *Lithuania.* When he returned to England, he had to establish another circle of friends to replace those he had alienated himself from. His frequent disgust at his own bodily impulses was equaled only by his horror of being alone. He found himself more and more drawn into the upper-class circle around Edward Marsh, as he met and became friends with the Asquiths (belying his attitude of only a few years before—Asquith "is a wicked worm" [*L,* 224]), Lady Eileen Wellesley, and, later, Marsh's political patron, Winston Churchill. Most important of these was Cathleen Nesbitt, who soon came to replace Noel Olivier as Brooke's idealized love object, a switch of allegiances that Noel was well aware of. Virginia Woolf noted in her 1923 diary that Noel Olivier told her, "And Rupert had gone with Cathleen Nesbitt & [Noel] had been jealous, & he had spoken against women & gone among the Asquiths and changed."[13] Even so, one portion of Brooke's personality did not change: he treated Nesbitt with ultimately the same noli me tangere attitude that he had used with Noel Olivier, but for a different reason; as he confessed later to Marsh, about Nesbitt's suitability as a wife, "Cathleen's character is very good, and I'm very fond of her. Why not her?—On the other hand, she's an actress" (*SOL,* 243, n.1). This, of course, was the same writer who condemned the Puritans for their hostile attitude toward the theater. (Significantly, in Barrie's original *Peter Pan,* Peter tells Wendy, "No one must ever touch me." And no one ever does.)[14]

Brooke fit in so well with this new circle of acquaintances that many of his former friends would later speculate (not without some Bloomsburian irony) that Brooke's real success, had he lived, would have come in politics. Brooke's greatest success at this time was certainly managerial, when Edward Marsh came up with the idea for a poetry anthology that would grow into the series *Georgian Poetry*. Brooke at this time also became closer with many of the contributors to that first volume of the series—Lascelles Abercrombie, Wilfred Gibson, and Edward Thomas, among others—and he gave the first reading at Harold Monro's Poetry Bookshop. Many of these poets (including the expatriate Robert Frost) were located in and around the small Gloucestershire village of Dymock, and Brooke enthusiastically joined in their plan to publish a small series of collections, eventually to be titled *New Numbers*. While Brooke was becoming more well known in poetic circles, his work was still not as widely read as that of the other contributors, and he thus jumped at the chance, as he told his mother: "Rather a score for me, as my 'public' is smaller than any of theirs!" (*L,* 484). To Gibson he confessed—in an underappreciated aspect of his personality, his self-deprecating humor—that his first contribution to *New Numbers* would be "Oh, Dear! oh, Dear! A Sonnet" (*L,* 486).

To Tahiti

While Brooke was becoming more successful artistically, he was also becoming more settled about the shape of his academic career. He rewrote and resubmitted his dissertation and won his fellowship at King's. Yet in the midst of this success, he decided to embark on a series of travels that would eventually take him halfway around the world. To some of Brooke's newer friends, it might have seemed like a sudden decision, but he had been mulling over some sort of journey ever since he had semirecovered from Lulworth, and his closest friends, particularly Frances Cornford, had urged him to go to America and engage in some kind of physical labor, both for mental therapy and to distance himself physically from Cox. Still, the likelihood of Rupert Brooke's becoming a migrant farm worker is about as imaginable as T. S. Eliot's becoming a cab driver, and Brooke eventually arranged to go to the United States and Canada as a journalist for the *Westminster Gazette,* participating in the by now traditional genre of British literary personalities writing about their experiences in America, a genre that included works by Charles Dickens, Frances and Anthony Trollope, and Oscar Wilde. By the time he left, the putative physiotherapeutic benefits of his trip had been long forgotten, but the idea of avoiding Cox was still an important consideration. As he told Nesbitt, somewhat out of a clear blue sky, "I do love you so: and yet I'm going to leave England in May. I've got to go, for a bit. Because I promised. I got mixed up with a woman" (*L*, 455). The emotional aftermath of their affair was so devastating to both Brooke and Cox that they both had to leave England for various periods (Cox, for instance, went to Russia) to avoid running into each other.

During the first section of Brooke's travels, he had to face one of his worst fears: loneliness. While some of this phobia emerges in the accounts that were later collected into *Letters from America* and will be discussed later, one particular experience vividly spilled over into his letters and gives a clue to the psychic journey he was also undertaking. In Canada he made a side trip up an otherwise undistinguished river, the Saguenay. To Brooke, however, it was a river out of the *Inferno,* as he told Nesbitt: "Then I noticed the face of the river was queer, and as I watched it, I began to think I could see things coming out of it—large black things you know—I don't know what—turning and looking at you and bellying—so I came and shut myself in here, in my cabin, and read Jane Austen" (*L*, 480). A further descriptive phrase in the article on the same experience gives an additional clue: "I found that under a prolonged gaze the face of the river began to writhe and eddy, as if from some horrible suppressed emotion."[15] He had also told Nesbitt earlier in the same letter, using his most infamous "unpleasant" metaphor from "Channel Passage," that after a bout of homesickness, "I threw up a lot of slobby old memories" (*L*, 480). By placing himself in a situation where, for the first time in his life, he was removed from the circles (little wonder that Dante came to mind here) of family, school, and friends he had used to insulate himself from himself, Brooke was attempting to purge himself of what he perceived as the weaknesses in his character. In the end, he was only partly successful, for instead of letting those monsters emerge and confronting them, he retreated into more ordered dreams of a secular paradise.

Since Brooke's income was limited during his travels, to continue them he often had to borrow money from literary people he met. After traveling steadily westward through Canada, he decided he would continue his journey in that direction, moving on to Hawaii and eventually the South Seas. During his ocean voyages Brooke wrote several works, including "Clouds" and "One Day," and at Hawaii "A Memory" and "Waikiki," all of which reveal him deliberately trying to expunge his

painful memories of Ka Cox and Noel Olivier. He seems to have been
somewhat successful, for his subsequent correspondence with them has a
more detached and objective tone. Many of his other more uncomfortable propensities, however, persisted and even hardened. He insulted a
Jewish passenger on board ship after he read about the Marconi scandal
(as well as resigning from the Liberal Club because of its Jewish members). He complained, in a somewhat playful vein, that the sight of
Niagara Falls had caused him to adopt a philosophy he had long rejected: "I'm afraid I'm a Victorian at heart, after all. . . . For I sit and stare at
the thing and have the purest Nineteenth Century grandiose thoughts,
about the Destiny of Man, the Irresistibility of Fate, the Doom of
Nations, and the fact that Deaths awaits us All, and so forth.
Wordsworth Redivivus. Oh dear! Oh dear!" (L, 491). And in his writings
to his idealized female correspondents, he began emphasizing a new
attribute that had become crucial in his personal relationships: goodness.
To the Marchesa Capponi, an Englishwoman he had met in the United
States, he was soon writing as if she were Cathleen Nesbitt or Noel
Olivier: "There are only two things in the world I think beautiful. One
is a woman's head and body, and the other is goodness" (L, 511). When
he wrote similarly to Nesbitt later, "I adore you. I love you in every other
way: and I worship the goodness in you" (L, 617), she confessed in her
memoirs, "But when he would go on to say I was beautiful and 'divinely
good' . . . my heart sank a little. How could anyone measure up to the
dreams he had fabricated?"[16]

Brooke's idealization of women was intimately bound up with his
growing antipathy toward another group which he felt was weakening
the moral fabric of society: the feminists. Such prejudices began to affect
his literary judgments. Like many other youthful literati in the early part
of this century, he had been an ardent Ibsenite; now he claimed that "the
morbid symptom of lovelessness is that denial of sex called feminism,
with its resultant shallowness of women and degradation of man," and
that "its apostle" was "a great and dirty playwright, Ibsen" (PRB,
176–77). In a depressed moment of self-analysis he had admitted to Cox
that he felt his own poetic gifts came from his mother's intense desire to
have a girl after her second child, a daughter, had died young: "while the
mother was thinking of the daughter another child was born, and it was
a son, but in consequence of all this very female in parts—sehr dichter-
isch—me" (L, 375). Yet now he blamed the ills of the modern world on
this admixture of masculine and feminine (the infamous "half-men" of
the war sonnet "Peace"): "if feminists are 'women' trying to be men, I

suppose 'men' trying to be women are hominists" (*L,* 592). In Chicago on his way back to Europe, he reportedly gave an impassioned outburst on the topic; the photographer Eugene Hutchinson described Brooke's harangue this way: "this mixture of the sexes was all wrong. . . . [M]ale was male and female was female and any intermingling of the two was morbid and calamitous. In other words, this Shelleylike youth with his hypersensitive face and girlish smoothness of skin and his emotional blue eyes was trying to tell us that manliness in men was the one hope of the world."[17] It is unclear at this point whether Brooke still felt that he himself was "very female in parts," but Hutchinson's emphasis on the incongruity of Brooke's declaration with his own physical appearance reveals why Brooke reacted so intensely to the topic. At the same time, he was vain about the effect he had on people; as Leonard Woolf noted, when women were present Brooke adopted "the attitude of the farmyard cock around the hens" (L. Woolf, 19). Brooke himself ruefully confessed that this aspect of his character clashed with his moral attitudes: "My subconscious is angry with every dreary young woman I meet, if she doesn't fall in love with me: and my consciousness is furious with her if she does" (*L,* 611). (The terminology Brooke uses here to describe himself refutes the idea that Brooke was "cut off by philosophy and correctness from any direct knowledge of psychology.")[18]

In his continual quest for a secular heaven, Brooke ended up in the South Seas and Tahiti, where, as most of his biographers agree, he found the greatest peace he was able to achieve in his life. Much of this he describes in images bound up with one of his favorite themes, youth, and in terms reminiscent of Brooke's favorite celebration of eternal youth, *Peter Pan,* and its Mermaids' Lagoon: "It's getting back to one's childhood, somehow: but not to the real childhood, rather to the childhood that never was, but is portrayed by a kindly sentimental memory; a time of infinite freedom, no responsibility, perpetual play in the open air, unceasing sunshine, never-tiring limbs, and a place where time is not, and supper takes place at breakfast-time and breakfast in the afternoon, & life consists of expeditions by moonlight and diving naked into waterfalls and racing over white sands beneath feathery brooding palm-trees" (*L,* 530–31). While in Tahiti, he also entered into what would be the most physically satisfying of his relationships with women. To Brooke's more protective biographers, this Tahitian woman, Taamata, was "a native girl of rare grace and intelligence," and "the two of them were intimate friends," while it is decorously claimed that reportedly "she was a daughter of the chief" (Hassall, 431); however, other biographers aver a hum-

bler station for her: "it would be unfair to call her a prostitute" (Delaney,
206). The latter view was closer to the truth, based on a letter from her to
Brooke much later, after he had returned to England: "Whe have good
times all girls in Papeete have good times whit Argentin boys" (*L*, 653,
n.1). While this elevation of Taamata is an interesting example of how
Brooke's guardians defend his reputation (the one woman with whom he
was able to sustain a physical relationship without throwing himself into
paroxysms of guilt must have been of noble blood), the important fact is
that Brooke was able to a certain extent to heal himself; as Delaney has
perceptively noted, one of Brooke's most important images is transformed in his best poem written in Tahiti: "Water washed away sex; it
was the element of purity, even when he bathed naked with Noel or
Bryn. But in the lagoon at Mataia bodies plunged to be united" (Delaney,
207). As Brooke asked Violet Asquith, "[H]ow can one know of heaven
on earth and not come back to it?" (*L*, 543).

War

Brooke, however, eventually realized that he had to leave heaven and
return to England; on other trips before, he'd often confessed to a patriotic love for England that was, according to him, merely the result of his
absence from it. Added to this habitual emotion now was the patriotism
beginning to grow in him as a reaction against all the pernicious influences he saw in modern culture. He wrote to Raverat that Samuel
Johnson was "the only man I love. An Englishman, by God" (L 580).
And he also felt that he had accomplished his psychological goals; as he
wrote in a disingenuously self-pitying vein to Marsh, "The Game is Up,
Eddie. . . . I've lost a dream or two. I tried to be a poet. And because I'm
a clever writer, & because I was forty times as sensitive as anybody
else—I succeeded a little. . . . I am what I came out here to be—Hard.
. . . I'll never be able to write anything more, I think. Or perhaps I can
do plays of a sort—I think I'll have to manage a theatre" (L , 568).
While this letter has been held up as proof that Brooke had been
"healed," it is also just as much an attempt to elicit approval from Marsh
by overemphasizing certain emotional states. Brooke had become "hard"
in many of the worst ways. Perhaps his most offensive letter is one puta-
tively written to Helena Cornford, the six-month-old daughter of two of
his closest friends, in which he "revealed" to her that he would be dreaming of a return to the South Seas, while at the same time in London
"another Jew has bought a peerage . . . and the ways are full of lean &

vicious people, dirty, hermaphrodites and eunuchs, Stracheys, moral vagabonds, pitiable scum" (*L*, 573). He warned her that America and New Zealand "are countries ruled by women. . . . Helena, do not, as you grow even older, become a feminist: become, I pray you, a woman" (*L*, 574). His puritanism might have been temporarily mollified in Tahiti, but his paranoia remained unassuaged.

Brooke returned to England in June 1914. Since the idea of sex without marriage after his affair with Cox was abhorrent to him (unless he was removed from indigenous restraints), and he realized he was at the same time driven by his sexual impulses, he felt compelled to get married: "One can't—I can't—be properly and permanently all right till I'm married. . . . Marrying without love seems like shutting an irrevocable door on all that matters" (*L*, 402). The domestic happiness of close friends like the Raverats and Cornfords that had once seemed to him to represent a loss of freedom now began to fill him with jealousy and melancholy. As he wrote to Raverat, "One hangs hopelessly around young women one doesn't care for a scrap, and—at this date—sees through entirely. . . . All very dull. Wish to God I was married" (*L*, 595). Also on his return he felt much closer to many subjects and people against which he had formerly rebelled, not the least of which was his mother: as he told Marsh, "I have to be at Rugby a good deal when I return. I've such a warmth for the Ranee" (L , 590). He had grown much more affectionate toward England during his absence, that habitual attitude of his which he had gently satirized before in one of the original titles to "Grantchester": "The Sentimental Exile." Now his fondness for England held little irony, as in this description from a letter, reminiscent of the coda to Forster's *Howards End:* "The last few days here have been glorious, and the air is so heavy (but not sleepy) with the scent of hay and mown grass and roses and dews and a thousand wild flowers that I'm beginning to think of my South Sea wind [as] pale and scentless by comparison!" (*L*, 594). And he had finally achieved a level of balance and self-realization in his emotions and communications with Cox: "I only know that—inevitably or not—through me you have been greatly hurt, and two or three years of your life—which can be so wonderful—have been changed and damaged. And I'm terribly ashamed before you. . . . Till I think you're complete, I shan't be happy" (*L*, 614–15).

Since 1912 Brooke, along with many other thinking persons in Europe, had been expecting a possible European war. During these years he had visualized himself going to the conflict as a journalist. He had expressed some reservations about Germany—"The Germans are nice, &

well-meaning, & they try; but they are SOFT" (*L,* 300)—but these were
in a jocular vein, and semiserious. As war became imminent, he told
friends that he believed autocratic Russia was as great an evil as
Germany: "Prussia is a devil. And Russia means the end of Europe and
any decency" (*L,* 603). Unlike the common perception of him as a consistently jingoistic sloganeer, Brooke was initially despondent when war
was first declared. He grew into his more patriotic beliefs over the eight
months he was alive during the war. Since he was unable to obtain a
position as war correspondent, he, like many other members of the intelligentsia in both of Britain's major wars in this century, attempted to
find some government post that could employ his talents; like most of
them, he was unsuccessful. As he told Lady Eileen Wellesley, "I wanted
to use my intelligence. I can't help feeling I've got a brain. I thought
there must be some organizing work that demanded intelligence. But,
on investigation, there isn't" (*L,* 608). In the same letter he confessed
that he thought his attempt to become a journalist while others were
ready to risk their lives was essentially unworthy, "base," and he blamed
it on that part of his personality which he had elsewhere condemned as
"vagabond": "But the other half is a wanderer and a solitary, selfish,
unbound, and doubtful. Half of my heart is of England, the rest is looking for some home I haven't yet found. . . . It was that part, I suppose,
which, when the tumult & unrest in me became too strong, sent me
seeking for a correspondentship" (*L,* 608). His former Bloomsbury
friends, so many of whom were to become conscientious objectors,
earned only his contempt: "dehumanized, disgusting people. They are
mostly pacifists and pro-Germans. I quarrel with them twice a day" (*L,*
613). When he was complimented for enlisting, he could only wonder at
the tone of it: "Of course, the imputation that a Cambridge poet might
be expected to funk, is rather beastly, and fairly true" (*L,* 643).

Brooke's first attempt to enlist involved joining with his Cambridge
Fabian friend Ben Keeling one of the OTC units associated with the Inns
of Court. Brooke did not intend to remain with the unit long, however,
and soon he was able to have some strings pulled through the Marsh-
Churchill connection and join the Royal Naval Division as a sublieu-
tenant. Keeling, echoing the later criticisms of such enlisted writers as
Ivor Gurney, disgustedly wrote, "Rupert Brooke has dropped out. He
wants a commission after all, and thinks he can get one through pushing
in various quarters."[19] Brooke's socialism, it seemed to Keeling, did not
extend to serving with the people whose conditions he wished to
improve. At any rate, Brooke was soon in training and offhandedly

spouting remarks that revealed the schoolboy bravado that would form the basis for the Brooke countermyth: "Well, if Armageddon is on, I suppose one should be there" (Hassall, 459); "Come and die. It'll be great fun" (*L,* 655). Brooke was adopting another pose, this one again lifted from his favorite play: as Peter Pan exclaims, "(*with a drum beating in his breast as if he were a real boy at last*). To die will be an awfully big adventure" (Barrie, 61). Brooke also felt, as did many others in this time of crisis, an even more compelling need to get married, as he told Raverat: "How divine to have even a few hours of what the rest of life is a grey pre-existence to—marriage: with, oh! *anybody.* But how dreadful to return from Berlin to a partner for Eternity whom one didn't particularly *want*" (*L,* 656). Yet no matter how urgent this drive seemed to him, there was little danger of his finding any suitable woman until he had attained a more mature and realistic outlook.

Crusading

The Royal Naval Division soon enough found its way into combat, and the event deeply affected most of Brooke's pronouncements on the war, including the war sonnets. Samuel Hynes's declaration that "Poor Brooke never got past the self-glorifying stage, because he did not get to the war"[20] is an unfair but typical example of the criticism that has been made of Brooke's war experience. The Royal Naval Division was sent to Belgium to assist in holding the Channel ports. Instead, the soldiers found themselves involved in the evacuation of Antwerp. They were fired on and shelled, briefly held some trenches, and then retreated with a large number of civilian refugees. Apprehensive about his control over his "nerves" since the Lulworth episode, Brooke was pleased to discover that his reactions seemed to show that he was physically courageous. But more crucial was his emotional response to what was initially called (and later sarcastically referred to as) the rape of Belgium. Since so much propagandistic exaggeration—nuns raped, babies bayoneted—was made by authorities at the time, the reaction against it has blurred the tragedies that did occur. Brooke was level-headed and objective about what he saw: "The Germans have behaved fairly well in the big cities. But the policy of bullying had been carried out well. And half a million people preferred homelessness and the chance of starvation, to the certainty of German rule" (*L,* 632). In the same letter he spoke of the "Dantesque Hell" of marching through a landscape illuminated by tens of thousands of gallons of gasoline ignited to prevent their falling into German hands, but to him the "truer Hell" was the immense number of refugees who fled from the Germans. This became his Cause, what he termed "one of the greatest crimes of history" (L, 632–33). The charge has, of course, been made that Brooke nevertheless did not live to experience the drawn-out attrition that trench warfare on the Western front would become, and he does declare once again that "It's a great life, fighting, while it lasts," yet he did foresee in this letter (written, ironically, four years to the day before the armistice was signed) that war would now be "half the youth of Europe blown through pain to nothingness, in the incessant mechanical slaughter of these modern battles. I can only marvel at human endurance" (L, 633). Underneath Brooke's ebullient bravado lay a capacity to become enlarged by his new experiences.

On Brooke's return to England, he wrote over the Christmas holidays the poems that were to make, expand, and ultimately explode his reputation: the "1914" sonnets. Brooke had been transferred to the Hood battalion, where, along with the son of the prime minister, "Oc" Asquith, and an old Rugby friend, Denis Browne, he prepared for Winston Churchill's plan to wrest Constantinople from the Turks, free the Black Sea, and open the Russian ports: the disastrous Gallipoli campaign. To evade the censors, many of these classically trained junior officers loaded their correspondence with literary allusions about their destinations, and Brooke eagerly lapsed into the miles gloriosus stance again as he declared to Violet Asquith, "I suddenly realize that the ambition of my life has been—since I was two—to go on a military expedition against Constantinople"; however, a few sentences later he conceded, "This is nonsense" (L, 662–63), a disclaimer Brooke's critics neglect when presenting this boast as evidence of his naivete. Brooke more objectively admitted to Ward that the battalion realized full well what would happen to them on the beaches when they landed: "But when we do get out, [the Hood] will be used to break the enemy lines by numbers à l'Allemagne: so that's why they expect 75% casualties" (L, 652). Even if Brooke did not live to participate in Western front battles with mind-numbing casualty rates like those of the Somme, he was fully cognizant of the dangers that would be involved in attempting to take a beachhead protected by troops equipped with twentieth-century weaponry.

The Hood was prepared for a landing in early April that had to be postponed, so the battalion went to Egypt. There, in another instance of string-pulling (this time not at Brooke's request), the commanding general, Sir Ian Hamilton, offered Brooke a staff appointment, which he refused for several reasons: a feeling of camaraderie with his friends and his troops; a reluctance to leave them short-staffed before such a difficult operation (as he wrote to his mother, "it wouldn't be very fair to my company to leave it suddenly at the last moment like this, with a gap it couldn't fill, out here" [*L*, 681]), and a probably equal unwillingness to appear a shirker in escaping such a risky operation. He was prepared to accept Hamilton's proposal after the battle, as he admitted to Marsh with a characteristic appraisal: a staff appointment "might be fun, after a campaign in my present capacity" (*L*, 680). Brooke's mood, pessimistic since the beginning of the war, now became fatalistic, as he tried to arrange his affairs in the event of his death. His letters to Cox became valedictions; she was the closest he had to a widow, he told her, and attempted to make a final peace with her: "My dear, my dear, you did me wrong: but I have done you very great wrong. Every day I see it greater" (*L*, 669). He instructed Ward to destroy all correspondence from two women correspondents, including Lady Eileen Wellesley, and any other letters that their writers asked. In a passage of immense irony, considering the later attempts to protect his reputation, he adjured Ward to "let [the public] know the poor truths" (*L*, 671). He asked that Marsh be his literary executor and, in a romantic gesture that ensured the survival of his myth immediately after the war, named the poets Walter de la Mare, Wilfred Gibson, and Lascelles Abercrombie to be his heirs. To Marsh he admitted, "I wish I'd written more. I've been such a failure" (*L*, 669), but that slim poetic output he termed a failure would make his heirs financially independent.

Apotheosis

While engaging in the typical round of sightseeing activities of any visitor to Egypt, Brooke fell ill with several maladies, including sunstroke and dysentery. Brooke's immune system, never inherently strong, had been previously weakened in Tahiti when a foot injury he received became infected. Back on board ship, Brooke grew ill again, this time apparently from an insect bite (the countermyth speculates that it was an inflammation from a venereal disease). At this time he learned from a *Times* article Marsh had sent him that Dean Inge, in his Easter sermon at St. Paul's on the resurrection, had held out as an exemplum "The Soldier," the last of Brooke's war sonnets, saying that "the enthusiasm of a pure and elevated patriotism had never found a nobler expression" (Hassall, 502); however, Brooke's speculations on the afterlife as "a pulse in the eternal mind" were not, to the dean, congruent with Christian dogma or the text the dean had used from Isaiah. Denis Browne wrote to Marsh that Brooke "was sorry that Inge didn't think he was as good as Isaiah" (*L,* 684). They were to be his last reported remarks. He died—as many were to see as appropriate—on 23 April, St. George's and Shakespeare's day. He was buried in a grave in a peaceful site on the island of Skyros, which he had visited before his death. His epitaph read in Greek that he was "the servant of God . . . Who died for the deliverance of Constantinople from the Turks" (Hassall, 512). It was a fitting capstone to a life already entering legend, and even nonsubscribers to the myth were affected by it; Wilfred Owen, for instance, carried a photograph of the grave in his copy of *1914 and Other Poems.*[21]

The flurry of telegraphs and radiograms from General Hamilton, Churchill, and the prime minister surrounding Brooke's death were the beginning of his secular canonization. That almost all of his other friends from the Hood battalion died during the Gallipoli expedition both added to his symbolic value and necessitated his elevation to iconic status. (His younger brother, Alfred, died on the Western front not even two months after Brooke.) The evolution—and devolution—of Brooke's reputation will be more fully investigated in the last chapter. The immediate tributes to Brooke in the national press were led by first Marsh and then Churchill and represented the two main directions the myth-making would take: the personal and the official. Churchill's tribute concluded: "Joyous, fearless, versatile, deeply instructed, with classic symmetry of mind and body, he was all that one would wish England's noblest sons to be in days when no sacrifice but the most precious is acceptable, and the most precious is that which is most freely proffered" (Hassall, 515). The myth was initially necessary both to those who had to justify ordering so many men to their deaths and to those survivors who, like Brooke's mother, had to seek their own reconciliation for what had happened to their loved ones. Brooke had written a few months before his death, "The central purpose of my life, the aim and the end of it, now, the thing God wants of me, is to get good at beating Germans. That's sure. But that isn't what it was. What it was, I never knew, and God knows I never found" (*L,* 631). In the deepest irony of all, after his life was over, in the use that was made of the circumstances of his death, Rupert Brooke found his true vocation.

Chapter Two

Brooke's Poetry

Readers of Geoffrey Keynes's edition of *The Poetical Works* of Brooke,[1] initially published in 1946, will be immediately struck by Keynes's unusual arrangement of the poems in reverse chronological order, with the exception of some fragments Brooke wrote en route to the Dardanelles in 1915. In his edition Keynes has added 38 previously unpublished poems to the 82 originally included in *Poems* (1911) and *1914 and Other Poems,* some of them of little intrinsic merit or interest, perhaps with less justification than Anthony Thwaite's controversial additions to the *Collected Poems* of Philip Larkin. The effect of such an arrangement gives the appearance of protecting, or at least admitting the lesser value of, Brooke's earliest works. It tacitly—almost implicitly—gives credence to the theory that Brooke's main poetic appeal lies in his legend, which is inextricably linked to the later poems: the myth endorses the work. Keynes's strategy is reminiscent of what has now become a cliché in the organization of biographies, to begin with the death of one's subject, particularly since the first poem in *The Poetical Works* is "Fragment" (which is separated from Brooke's other final fragments, which are placed at the end of the volume). This poem ends with the proleptic phrase "soon to die / To other ghosts—this one, or that, or I" (*PW,* 17), allowing no reader to forget that the writer of these lines did die soon after. Of course, a reader can begin at the end of the volume and work through to the beginning, but even that strategy does not remove the impression of a poetic life viewed through the wrong end of the telescope.

Prizewinner

Two of Brooke's longest sustained poetical works are "The Pyramids" and "The Bastille," poems written to set historical themes for the poetry competition at Rugby. (The latter won first place, while the other received a *proxime accessit.*) Since Brooke is attempting in these works for the most part to reproduce an attitude that would win a prize, many of the themes and expressions in these poems are not only derivative, but uncharacteristically derivative. Some ideas Brooke explores here are worth noting, however, both those which are unique to these works and those which foreshadow certain directions Brooke's work would take.

Both poems are studded with themes and tropes connected to the decadent phase Brooke was exploring in his private poetry of the time, but most of these are underplayed, since the judges of a school contest would not look favorably on such a pose were it extravagantly expressed. Thus, the Sphinx in "The Pyramids" is more reminiscent of that at Giza than that of St. John Lucas (who wrote a novel called *The Marble Sphinx*). "The gloom that men call Death" (*PW*, 190) awaits all in "The Pyramids," and "Summer . . . Languid with roses" (*PW*, 174) takes place unknown to those trapped in "The Bastille": both images are from decadence, but conventional views more often prevail in these works. The climax of "The Pyramids," for instance, invokes "The Eternal Music that God makes" (*PW*, 193), obviously a concession by the unbelieving Brooke to the pieties of the judges. Despite such genuflections, however, one cannot assume, as does Ronald Pearsall, that other aspects of the poems, such as "The eternal day" in "The Bastille" (*PW*, 179), represent "a Christian eternity, something that would be acceptable to the judges of the contest" (Pearsall, 27). "The Bastille" concludes with the declaration "Men shall be Gods" (*PW*, 179), an unmistakably non-Christian sentiment, an affirmation of the serpent's promise to Eve in Genesis. This vision of a utopian future is more revealing of the political themes Brooke explores in these poems, themes that, for all of Brooke's political involvement, he rarely explores or expresses elsewhere in his poetry.

The main thrust of "The Pyramids," besides the standard meditations on the evanescence of human life, is the ultimate ephemerality of political empires: Egyptian, Greek, Roman, and, though never stated, that of the British Empire. Lives have been wasted "In the vain merciless mad race / For dreams of 'Empire' and 'Supremacy'" (*PW*, 191). Such a stance in 1904 was somewhat unusual for an English public school boy to adopt; although Brooke's beliefs on empire are never clearly stated elsewhere, he seems to have been a "little Englander," his patriotism, like Belloc's, not extending beyond the British isles. In "The Bastille" he confronts the political problem of revolution. His image for that upheaval is traditional: the darkness inside the Bastille will yield to "the slow inevitable day" of revolution (*PW*, 177); a political poster Brooke would have seen later, in Ben Keeling's room, for instance, was titled "Forward the Day Is Breaking." Much of the other imagery in the poem is traditional, but in its last section Brooke makes a prescient remark: the dreams of the French Revolution, as viewed from the perspective of 1905, have faded, "For we know / Not by one sudden blow / Are peace and freedom won" (*PW,* 178). This declaration shows that Brooke was at least ready to accept the Fabian philosophy of gradual socialism. The poem's final vision of "The eternal day," far from being Christian, is the heaven on earth of socialism, "sin and bondage past" (*PW,* 179), because the reasons for such evils—"Grey poverty" and "tyrannous Wealth" (*PW,* 178)—will have been removed. While the radicalism of these poems is mild, they provided two of the few opportunities for Brooke to assert such ideas poetically. In later life he reportedly wanted to write a long poem on modern economic conditions that would climax in a depiction of revolution but gave up on it. As the weaknesses of these prize poems show, Brooke was essentially a miniaturist; most of the longer works he attempted gave him some difficulty, particularly in matters of tone.

Decadent

Many of the early poems Keynes added to *The Poetical Works* are eminently forgettable, evocative of no other writer; the decadent poems, while derivative, at least indicate some of the characteristic subjects Brooke would continue to write about. Since decadence is in part a reaction to Victorian sincerity, most of the emotions appearing in these poems are artificial, almost patently unauthentic, as are those emotions when they appear in the writings Brooke was imitating. One of the decadents' principal subjects is a morbid concern with death. As Pearsall points out, "The death note of Decadent writing caught thousands of hearts at the turn of the century. . . . But it seldom sticks as it stuck to Brooke" (Pearsall, 29). Much of Brooke's preoccupation with mortality arises out of an adolescent fixation on death as a means of escape, intimately bound up with the posture of being unable to forget painful memories. The death of the earth, for instance, is described in fin de siècle terms reminiscent of the last chapters of H. G. Wells's *The Time Machine:* "Quenching the light . . . And bringing back the terrible night that was" (*PW,* 186); the soul of the dead must face "the darkness that is God" (*PW,* 171). The possibility of old age becomes an object of intense fear in these poems, and youth the subject of worship.

Youthful beauty is often described in floral images, with homoerotic overtones: "flesh more fair than pale lilies" (*PW,* 182). Lilies become the emblematic flower in these poems, betokening everything but their traditional association with resurrection. The title flowers in "The Lost

Lilies," the symbol of dimly evoked, forbidden passion, are contrasted
with the other favorite flower in these poems, "the roses' purple kiss";
the speaker in the poem mourns for "The immortal pallor of my lost
lilies" (PW, 172–73). Paleness, languor, a studied enervation—all the
poses Brooke absorbed from Wilde and Ernest Dowson are here. Some
of these affectless exercises, however, do spring into life at times when
Brooke engages certain emotions and strategies. The poem "In January"
is the first hint of what has been called Brooke's later realism: the speaker declares he has not forgotten "The dripping bough: the sad smell of
the rotten / Leaves," but the poem ends more conventionally as the
speaker also remembers "A glorious light" (PW, 187). "Song of the
Beasts" is an outgrowth of Brooke's antisensualism, covertly celebrating
that which it condemns. As its epigraph states, *Sung, on one night, in the
cities, in the darkness,* the song is a combination of Dr. Hyde and Dr.
Moreau: "Have you not felt the quick fires that creep / Through the hungry flesh, and the lust of delight, / And hot secrets of dreams that day
cannot say?" In another twisting of Genesis, the speaker declares, "Ye are
men no longer, but less and more, Beast and God" (PW, 168). The poem
concludes as the speaker leads the rest of the beasts, lemming-like, out of
the city "To the black unresting plains of the calling sea" (PW, 169), an
image derived from the ambiguous comfort the ocean provides in such
poems as Matthew Arnold's "Dover Beach."

Perhaps the poem that best foreshadows Brooke's later concerns is
"The Beginning," in which the speaker promises to look for his beloved
one day, remembering the "Touch of your hands and smell of your hair."
Yet when they do meet that day, the speaker will "curse the thing that
once you were, / Because it is changed and pale and old" (PW, 166). This
represents an interesting contrast to Brooke's later, more famous attacks
on old age in "Menelaus and Helen," since here the speaker turns around
and curses the beloved for having the potential to grow old. While the
poem ends more conventionally, as the speaker admits the beloved will
also grow "old and wise," it is important because it introduces Brooke's
continuing war against time, which would culminate in his attempt to
freeze it in moments encapsulated like those in "Dining-Room Tea."

While decadence gave Brooke a tradition he could explore and build
on, more important, it gave him a series of conventions he could rebel
against, just as decadence itself was a revolt against Victorian sensibilities. One can see the more mature Brooke emerge gradually during
1907, the year in which he later said the young poet he had been "died."
"The Call," according to Christopher Hassall, was written (February

1907) about the death of his older brother, Richard, but this biographical connection is difficult to perceive under all the conventional decadent language: "I'll write upon the shrinking skies / The scarlet splendour of your name" (*PW,* 164). Perhaps the first poem fully in Brooke's mature, independent voice is the "Dawn," in which the matching first and last lines, "Opposite me two Germans snore and sweat" (*PW,* 162), indicate the direction Brooke's search for unconventional subject matter, particularly for the sonnet form, would take him—a subject matter later labeled "realistic," "ugly," or "unpleasant." Brooke's clearest declaration of poetic independence is the appropriately titled "Sonnet: in time of Revolt" (January 1908), written in defiance of his uncle Alan Brooke, dean of King's College, who had seemingly chided Brooke for using mild profanity. Brooke's seeming overreaction—"I am no boy! I AM / NO BOY!" (*PW,* 155)—is more understandable in light of his search for a wider subject matter for his verse, and the poem's last declaration—"So shall I curb, so baffle, so suppress / This too avuncular officiousness, / Intolerable consanguinity"—dimly echoes Stephen Dedalus's vow of "silence, exile, and cunning" as he resolves to break the ties of blood that bind him and also throws off the decadent posturings of the villanelle he writes in *A Portrait of the Artist as a Young Man.*[2] Although Brooke's experiments were never to approach Joyce's in depth, from now on Brooke's poetry would, on the whole, be an attempt to voice an original expression, not an echo.

Georgian

Brooke, even more than its editor, Edward Marsh, worked to puff and publicize the first volume of Marsh's anthology, *Georgian Poetry;* as he wrote to Marsh, "When I lie awake o'nights—as I sometimes do—I plan advertisements for 'Georgian Poets'" (*L,* 406), and he was constantly on the lookout for the volume in his travels in America and Canada, and distributed copies where none were available. Brooke also realized, however, that the concept of "Georgianism" in literature was a somewhat artificial construct of Marsh's; as he humorously noted, "And it's generally agreed that Marsh has got Georgianism on the brain, & will shortly issue a series of Georgian poker-work: & establish a band of Georgian cooks" (*L,* 597–98). Kenneth Millard has recently (1991) argued that Brooke was actually an Edwardian and that there really were no Georgians; however, Robert Ross in *The Georgian Revolt* (1965) and Myron Simon in *The Georgian Poetic* (1975) have more persuasively proven that Georgianism was an organized movement with its own coherent aesthetic, however much it appeared to spring full-blown out of one editor's taste, so to speak. Brooke himself argued that its very name betrayed it: it was "too staid for a volume designed as the herald of a revolutionary dawn."[3]

Of course, the chief problem with Georgian poetry is not its existence but its worth in the minds of critics, particularly after the World War I. Georgians in their time, as Ross and Simon show, were considered to be as iconoclastic and revolutionary as other, more identifiable premodernists; Georgians' works were marked, as Ross says, by "spiritual euphoria, a sense of vitality, anti-Victorianism, realism, and freedom of poetic diction. But most of these tendencies were not uniquely Georgian; they rather marked the Georgians, like the Imagists, Vorticists, and even Futurists, as scions of their age" (Ross, 237). Yet in 1918 T. S. Eliot was criticizing the Georgians for "pleasantness": "the Georgians caress everything they touch" (Ross, 160). Two events led to the general modern critical devaluation of the Georgians. The first was the attenuation of the poetic material Marsh published in anthologies after World War I. As Ross points out, "In 1912 and 1915 'Georgian' had implied vigor, revolt, and youth. After 1917 it was to imply retrenchment, escape, and enervation" (Ross, 165). The second was the sheer immense fact of the war itself. In *A War Imagined* Samuel Hynes has shown what an unbridgeable gulf the First World War meant to people in all walks of life, but particularly the arts.[4] Poets became divided into those who served and those who did not: Robert Graves, Siegfried Sassoon, and Wilfred Owen, however much antiwar their verse became, all still thought of themselves as Georgians, not as modernists. As the critical perception of the Georgians as poetic "dew-dabblers" solidified, their own attempts at artistic breakthroughs and boundary-extending were forgotten. Perhaps the most striking "forgotten" feature of the Georgian poets was their realism, and Brooke became briefly notorious for the few poems in his first volume, *Poems,* which concerned hitherto "unpoetic" subjects, when the public preferred, as did Marsh, "poetry that I can read at meals" (Hassall, 293).

The reasons behind Brooke's realistic approach are not entirely clear. There is a remnant of adolescent rebellion, and perhaps, as Ross speculates, it may have been part marketing ploy: "they attracted public attention" (Ross, 28). Others have postulated a more philosophical basis. Simon finds Brooke's realism rooted in the philosophical principles of Moore and Russell: "the Georgians acknowledged a real world, external to them, the existence of which was not contingent upon their perception of it. But that world was available for their inspection, and the first principle of their realism was that they must attend carefully to the concrete particulars of external experience."[5] The truth is somewhere in between the two explanations. Brooke's underlying psychological reason for the "ugliness" of certain of his poems is to shock, whether it be his mother; his uncle, the Dean of King's; the secretary to the lord of the admiralty, Edward Marsh; or, later, his former Cambridge friends. He is at the same time working through in his poetry his reaction to the philosophy of G. E. Moore he encountered with the Apostles, but he is not merely adapting or conforming to it. Some biographers have declared that Moore's principles provided Brooke with little inner strength when his psychic world began to crumble around him at Lulworth. Yet Brooke never really expected them to help; he was constantly using and testing Moorist postulates for his own agenda.

For instance, one of the most striking early realistic poems is "Wagner," a poem that has been grossly misread as being about the composer (Millard has mixed up Wagner's physical appearance with Rossini's).[6] Written at Queen's Hall in 1908, "Wagner" describes "the state of mind"—to use the famous Moorist touchstone—of a man "with a fat wide hairless face" who comes to listen to Wagner because "He likes love-music that is cheap" and "Likes women in a crowded place." As he hears the music, he fantasizes, "thinks himself the lover," because "He likes to feel his heart's a-breaking." The last stanza describes him externally, and he has obviously not been transfigured by his experience: "His little lips are bright with slime. . . . His pendulous stomach hangs a-shaking" (*PW,* 153). Brooke here questions the validity of such an artistic experience. Is a "state of mind" thus evoked by Wagner's music so as to induce dreams of romantic conquest and sorrow any less authentic, any less "good," than a more noble fantasy by a more prepossessing subject? If not, what of the state of mind of the poet who describes such an experience? In one of his most important letters, Brooke came close to answering these questions. Ben Keeling had written Brooke that he was becoming a pessimist, and Brooke attempted to dissuade him. Brooke called his solution either "mysticism or Life," and it consisted of viewing the world as it really was: "What happens is that I suddenly feel the extraordinary value and importance of everybody I meet, and almost everything I see. In *things* I am moved in this way especially by some things; but in people by almost all people. That is, when the mood is upon me. I roam about places . . . and sit in trains and see the essential

glory and beauty of all the people I meet. I can watch a dirty middle-
aged tradesman in a railway-carriage for hours, and love every dirty
greasy sulky wrinkle in his weak chin and every button on his spotted
unclean waistcoat. I know their states of mind are bad. But I'm so much
occupied with their being there at all, that I don't have time to think of
that" (L, 258). Of course, this was written in one of Brooke's own "optimistic" phases, in which he is close to the top of a manic mood swing. In
these moments Brooke was acutely aware of what he called "the
enchantment of being even for a moment alive in a world of real matter
(not that imitation, gilt stuff, one gets in Heaven) and actual people" (L,
260): quotidian matter and people are therefore appropriate subjects for
his poems, and by treating them he refutes Moore and his "states of
mind." "Wagner" is thus a kind of picture-within-a-picture; the fat man
"ignobly" appreciates Wagner, and Brooke "ignobly" appreciates the fat
man's appreciation.

Another aspect of Brooke's "realism" is its antiromanticism. Brooke
proffered this reason as a justification to Marsh when defending his most
notorious realistic poem, "A Channel Passage." In it a lover finds himself
becoming seasick on a channel ferry and, as a preventive, tries to recall
anything, but the only image that comes to mind is that of his lover:
"You, you alone could hold my fancy forever!" Such remembrance, however, leaves the speaker with only the choice of "A sea-sick body, or a
you-sick soul!" Instead of being a prophylactic, his lover's image acts as
an emetic, as he is wracked with "The sobs and slobbers of a last year's
woe" and vomits (PW, 113). Many critics have pointed out that the
poem is in itself weak, yet one assumes Brooke realized the undercutting
effect that the inverted word order of "up I throw" would have.
Complaining that such a dose of realism, "the brutality of human emotions," was necessary "after I've beaten vain hands in the rosy mists of
poets' experiences," Brooke invoked to Marsh the example of
Shakespeare's sonnet 130, "My mistress' eyes are nothing like the sun"
(L, 328). Brooke's main reason for writing "Channel Passage" seems to
have been to stake out his own territory, independent of Marsh and of
whatever other "dew-dabblers" were writing at the time. His most
unpleasant unpublished poem, for example, concerns a lover celebrating
his beloved's becoming the main course at a cannibal feast (preceding
Evelyn Waugh's Black Mischief by about 20 years); it was written in a letter from the South Seas to the daughter of the prime minister of
England, Violet Asquith (L, 541). Not for nothing was one of his papers
to the Apostles titled "Why Not Try the Other Leg?"

Beyond the rebellious playfulness inherent in these poems lies the deeper significance of this approach for Brooke: his attempt to demythologize romantic love by exploding its accompanying worship of the human body. Such a stance is inherent in the Shakespearean sonnet Brooke cites as his defense. It originates not only in that body-mistrusting portion of Brooke's psychological makeup which has been called, for want of a better term, his "puritanism," but also in the deep anxiety he perceived when he compared his own physical beauty to his own interior landscape, a self-hate that emerges in his litanies of "filthy, filthy," flung as much at himself as at the outer world. This is most strikingly brought out in his poems on the effects of age, which go far beyond the mild apprehension of the earlier poem "The Beginning." Chief among these later works is "Menelaus and Helen," a double sonnet initially inspired by a scene in Lucas's *The Marble Sphinx.* The first sonnet recapitulates the scene of conventional legend when Menelaus first confronts Helen after the fall of Troy; the picture here is of "The perfect Knight before the perfect Queen" (*PW,* 125)—which line, Brooke told Frances Cornford, "has a touch of the giggle behind it, perhaps in some lights" (*L,* 252). The second sonnet describes the aftermath of their *nostos,* their homecoming, as Helen grows into a shrew, and Menelaus a braggart, summed up in the half-line that is a sentence in both senses of the word: "And both were old" (*PW,* 125). They each come to forget their past glories in the senescence of old age, and the last line of the poem describes the only character in their legend who escaped such a fate, but only through early death: "And Paris slept on by Scamander side" (*PW,* 126). It is always tempting when writing about Brooke to overreact to what seems to be such an unerring personal prophecy, conflating Scamander with Skyros (as some do when they recount Brooke's pointing to the memorial wall of Rugby chapel and declaring, "They are keeping that for *me*"). Nevertheless, Brooke had just as keen an internal eye for what today would be called his "image" as any contemporary mass-media figure. "Menelaus and Helen" is Brooke's Georgian answer to the resolute Victorian virtues embodied in, for example, Tennyson's "Ulysses"; it also reveals Brooke's incapacity to visualize an inner beauty unconnected with the body's exterior appearance, no matter how hard he wishes the body would go away.

The same theme runs through "Jealousy," a poem so charged with emotion that one is driven to read it biographically. The speaker rails against his beloved for succumbing to the physical attractiveness of another: "the stupid bow / Of his red lips, and . . . the empty grace /Of

those strong legs and arms." The only consolation for the speaker is to
picture his beloved ruined by old age: "the thickening nose / And sweaty
neck and dulling face and eye / That are yours, and you, most surely, till
you die!" The duality that fascinates Brooke—that one inhabits one's
body yet is one's body—is encapsulated in that phrase, "That are yours,
and you." Nothing gives the speaker more satisfaction than imagining
his beloved and her lover in old age together, as she tends "A foul sick
fumbling dribbling body and old," as his lips, in a favorite word of
Brooke's, "can't hold slobber" (*PW,* 128). When that happens, the
speaker—and it is not too strong a word to use—rants, "And he'll be
dirty, dirty!" She, who is "lithe and free / And lightfoot," will "be dirty
too!" (*PW,* 129). The emotional energy expended in this outburst does
not seem to have been directed toward anyone in Brooke's life at the
time (1909), and when he indulged himself in depicting such emotions,
he was playing with a dangerous synergy that would be vented in the
aftermath of Lulworth.

Brooke's horror at the inevitable consequences of time on the human
body is part of what might be called his Platonic perspective on human
relationships, his hunger for the ideal, and the almost surreptitious relish
with which he describes "common & sordid things" (*L,* 328) that destroy
the ideal. Such is the situation in "The Voice," whose title recalls the earlier poem "The Call," which ended with the speaker and the caller
"clothed about with perfect love" (*PW,* 165). The setting in "The Voice"
is an outdoor scene, perhaps after a walk or during a camp-out, a situation Brooke increasingly came to depict in his poems. As the speaker
rests "Safe in the magic of my woods," he tries to puzzle out "the hidden
key / Of all that had hurt and puzzled me— / Why you were you" (*PW,*
132). His solitude is invaded by someone "Crashing and laughing and
blindly going," whose "Voice profan[es] the solitudes." This blunderer is
"you," the subject of his meditations, and as happened with Coleridge
and the person from Porlock, "The spell was broken, the key denied
me." The beloved's voice is not soothing and melodious but "quacked
beside me in the wood," giving rise to natural—but to the speaker, unin-
spiring—thoughts, such as, "'The sunset's pretty, isn't it?'" The speaker's
final reaction to this small talk is summed up in the last line of the
poem: "By God! I wish—I wish that you were dead!" Faced with this
detonation of hatred for someone who is, after all, only being human,
one is tempted to agree with Delaney, who views the poem biographically and claims, "However euphoric Brooke may have been at Bank, his
happiness seems to have rested on the lack of any real dialogue between

himself and his love," in this case, Noel Olivier, whom Delaney posits as the "you" of the poem (Delaney, 59). If so, what is then remarkable is that this poem was written for a contest in the *Westminster Gazette* for the best poem titled "The Voice"—and won. If this was a private emotion, Brooke certainly was not averse to sharing it widely. While Brooke's unpleasant poetry is partly fueled by internal psychic pressures, one must not forget that it was a public stance, carefully chosen in its infrequency for maximum shock value.

Some critics have found another influence operating on Brooke to create his "realism": his increasing interest in and passion for the poetry of John Donne. Not all Georgians viewed this as a healthy effect; John Drinkwater, for instance, blamed Brooke's "intellectual coldness" on "an immature enthusiasm for Donne's poetry."[7] Yet while Brooke at times certainly does appear to be attempting "metaphysical" associations in his poems, they often fall short, through lack of either distance ("The Voice") or aptness of ideas ("A Channel Passage"). Aside from a few important exceptions, he lacked the artistic stamina to work completely through an elaborate conceit, such as Donne did in "The Flea," a favorite of Brooke's. His best work in this vein is "Mummia," in which the speaker uses the examples of great lovers in art "To rarefy ecstasy," as, legend has it, lovers did when they "drank mummia," made from the dust of dead lovers, "To fire their limbs of lead." Such a conceit works for Brooke because he imagines the dead lovers surrounding the speaker and his beloved: "The unheard invisible lovely dead" (*PW,* 81). The dead here for Brooke affirm life: "And Life has fired, and Death not shaded, / All Time's uncounted bliss" (*PW,* 82).

Torn by his obsession with the duality of body and spirit, however, more often Brooke conceives the opposite situation: the lovers themselves as dead, bodiless. They look back on their lives, not realizing how duped they were by their desires. In "Dead Men's Love," written in the aftermath of Lulworth, two lovers, a poet and "A Woman like the Sun," have died but do not realize it. His songs have been quieted, but her body is "Dust, and a filthy smell." When they reunite in Hell, they realize, "with a sick surprise, / The emptiness of eyes" (*PW,* 83). Brooke wrote to Marsh later about this poem that "Hell just consists in such absence of bodies" (*L,* 361), but everything in the poem implies the converse: Hell is being doomed to rely on transient, tainted flesh to satisfy the needs of love. The poem "The Life Beyond" describes the afterlife in almost tautological terms: the dead lover is himself "a fly / Fast-stuck in grey sweat on a corpse's neck" (*PW,* 95). The conclusion of this sonnet reveals that the speaker's love has died, and the metaphor of the fly represents the speaker's existence as he carries on in the afterlife. And in "The Descent" the speaker has "left the mountain height" because his lover has called. Her body evokes predatory images—"white and hungry hands," a "troublous mouth"—and they end up losing their "human love between the mist and mire" (*PW*, 96). Brooke's suspicion and eventual conviction that the body is fated to corruption in every sense are relentless in these poems. The Shakespearean sonnet that looms behind Brooke's unpleasant poetry is not so much "My mistress' eyes" as that great paean to *pudor* (sexual shame), sonnet 129, "Th' expense of spirit in a waste of shame."

For Brooke, love, to be worthwhile and satisfying, must somehow become disembodied, and several of his poems describe that condition. In "Dust" the lovers have died, and while there is a Websterian tinge to the description of their corpses—"through the lips corruption thrust / Has stilled the labour of my breath" (*PW*, 100)—their afterlife is much cleaner: they will "dance as dust before the sun . . . and run / About the errands of the wind" (*PW*, 100). When two motes from each of them meet, they will have a similar effect on living lovers that the potion in "Mummia" has; only this inspiration, for Brooke, goes beyond the body:

> past desiring,
> So high a beauty in the air,
> And such a light, and such a quiring,
> And such a radiant ecstasy there. (*PW*, 101)

The motes will "pass, in light, to light . . . higher, higher" (*PW*, 101). While this description of love freed from carnality trails off into Brooke's persistent habit, which Marsh first noted, of substituting amorphous abstractions for concrete images, two other poems make this point more clearly, and further delineate Brooke's incipient Platonism.

One of these is the poem aptly entitled "Thoughts on the Shape of the Human Body." In a way it is an exercise, as Brooke tries to fill each line with a series of words: "but unsatisfied / Sprawling desires, shapeless, perverse, denied" (*PW*, 85). The reader must reconstruct the sense of the series of words, much as the speaker tries to descry meaning behind the "witless Fate" that governs human lives. The answer for the speaker is to be able to

Rise disentangled from humanity
Strange whole and new into simplicity,
Grow to a radiant round love, and bear
Unfluctuant passion for some perfect sphere. (*PW,* 85)

One searches in vain for a trace of irony, but Brooke is being inescapably serious here; this is Platonic love with a vengeance, with the music of the spheres tossed in. There is none of the self-knowing humor in, for instance, Donne's calling other couples "Dull sublunary lovers" in "A Valediction Forbidding Mourning." Brooke calmly, dispassionately presents a condition of perfect love, removed from the flow ("unfluctuant") of time. His "Sonnet (Suggested by some of the Proceedings of the Society for Psychical Research)" has been cited as an example of the Edwardian interest in such paranormal phenomena as a substitute for lost religious belief, but Brooke appears never to have pursued this alternative in his own life. Instead, the sonnet presents an opportunity for Brooke to investigate once again what a disincarnate love would involve: the dead lovers will realize "What this tumultuous body now denies; / And feel, who have laid our groping hands away; / And see, no longer blinded by our eyes" (*PW,* 40). In a sense this is Brooke's religion; it echoes the neo-Platonism of St. Paul's declaration in 1 Corinthians 13: "But when that which is perfect is come, then that which is in part shall be done away. . . . For now we see through a glass, darkly; but then face to face: now I know in part; but then shall I know even as also I am known." Perfect knowledge, attainable only through the sloughing off of the flesh, betokens the possibility of perfect love, when the lovers will "Learn all we lacked before" (*PW,* 40), an ambivalent phrase implying either that the lovers lacked knowledge or that they lacked freedom from their bodies.

Brooke's favorite trope for the perfectibility of love is thus the ghost; interestingly enough, as a boy he had a dream where "Afterwards I came back and haunted the house, causing much terror at a dinner party. The feeling of haunting is rather pleasing" (Hassall, 41). Yet one of his best poems reveals how such a vision was possible while one is still alive. "Dining-Room Tea" has often been cited as Brooke's principal Moorist "state-of-mind" poem. Its inspiration was a tea during one of the neo-pagans' camp-outs; present were some of the most important figures in Brooke's life: Justin Brooke, James Strachey, Geoffrey Keynes, and

Daphne, Bryn, and Noel Olivier (Ka Cox and Virginia Stephen were en route at the time)—"the changing faces that I loved," as the speaker calls them. The faces are changing because of the fitful illumination on them and because of "The light of laughter," and besides all these visual effects, they are changing because of the passage of time, "Proud in their careless transience." The poem revolves around the speaker's epiphany as he beholds "your innocence," presumably Noel Olivier's. This comprehension removes "the immortal moment" "From the dark woven flow of change" (*PW*, 110); the apprehender becomes almost divine in knowledge. All things previously caught up in time's flux are now fixed in place: "the fire's unglittering gleam, / The painted flame, the frozen smoke." His beloved becomes "august, immortal, white, / Holy and strange," and in one of Brooke's most effective paradoxical (one is tempted to say metaphysical) images, her whole being is "Freed from the mask of transciency" (*PW*, 111). But even though the speaker, like Faust, has asked this moment to stay, because it is so fair, time must begin again. The speaker's problem now becomes how to communicate this vision: "How could I cloud, or how distress, / The heaven of your unconsciousness?" (*PW*, 112). The tragedy for Brooke, not fully reflected in this poem, is that divine apprehension does not entail divine communion, which is why he elsewhere becomes so enraged at others' incomprehension of his own emotions. This Platonic poem, written about a circle of friends, ends circularly, recapitulating its first line as its last: "When you were there, and you and you" (*PW*, 112). The poem succeeds as much as the moment did in his life.

Brooke's other two most effective "metaphysical" poems involve similar imaginative leaps into characteristic concerns. "The Fish" describes a creature that eternally inhabits Brooke's favorite medium, water. The fish's milieu, "the clinging stream" (*PW*, 78), is related to Heraclitus's river, in which everything is flux and nothing remains still. The water for Brooke becomes emblem of the "fluctuant, mutable world" in which "shape to shape / Dies momently through whorl and hollow." The sensory impressions in it are the opposite of the frozen brilliances in "Dining-Room Tea": "Shaken translucency illumes / The hyaline of drifting glooms" (*PW*, 78). The fish's death is as limpid and obscure as his element as he "fades to some dank sufficient heaven" (*PW*, 79). Reminiscent of D. H. Lawrence's hymns to the unconscious, Brooke's poem compares this dim, primitive blood knowledge to human passions, and "the hands, the eyes of love!" The union of these body parts result in "The strife of limbs," and even if everywhere about them is "The infinite distance . . .

and vast around / The horizon," what remains for human lovers is "the sightless clinging." For the fish in his stream, "space is no more," and "The lights, the cries, the willows dim, / And the dark tide are one with him" (*PW*, 80). While the fish can only dimly see, he can more truly feel; humans, although capable of seeing, are blinded and doomed to "sightless clinging." The wit in this poem, while congruent with the language, is perhaps too heavy, too bound to the mistrust Brooke has for the physical, unlike Lawrence, who is triumphantly celebratory about similar subjects.

Lighter in treatment is the poem inspired by the fish's dream of that "dank sufficient" afterlife, "Heaven." Every idea Brooke has worked through in this sequence is treated with an ironic touch, all the more effective because it is ultimately directed at himself: "We darkly know, by Faith we cry, / The future is not Wholly Dry. / Mud unto mud!" In another anti-Victorian blast, he imagines a piscine deity "Who swam ere rivers were begun, / Immense, of fishy form and mind, / Squamous, omnipotent, and kind" (*PW*, 35). In his descriptions of the fish's paradise, Brooke is able once again to yoke opposites in Samuel Johnson's sense of the definition of metaphysical poetry: "mud celestially fair . . . Paradisal grubs are found; / Unfading moths, immortal flies, / And the worm that never dies" (*PW*, 36). To the fish the human emblem of death, "the worm that never dies," becomes the personification of bounty and largesse. In the mordant humor of this paradox, Brooke finally comes close to the effect Donne so often produced in his verse, chiefly through his distancing of the idea by first writing about it semisolemnly in "The Fish."

Brooke's only serious poem on religious themes is "Mary and Gabriel," a surprisingly lengthy (for Brooke) treatment of the Annunciation. Its uniqueness has prompted one critic to misread it: according to Pearsall, Brooke "had entered the hell period and was seeking for a religious identification as a means of getting out. This is a paranoid development as understood in psychiatry, and a desirable human development as understood in theology" (Pearsall, 124). Besides its muddling of religion and psychology, this analysis more crucially fails to take into account the most important omission in the poem: it is solely the account of the two title characters and never mentions God. In another of Brooke's frozen-moment poems, Gabriel is an androgynous messenger of the Ideal: "Not man's nor woman's was the immortal grace . . . lighting the proud eyes with changeless light" (*PW*, 62). The moment of conception is described in phrases reminiscent, as Pearsall points out, of Yeats's "Leda and the Swan": "She felt a trembling stir /

Within her body, a will too strong for her / That held and filled and mastered all" (*PW,* 62). The only problem is that Yeats's poem was published some 11 years after Brooke's. In another example of Brooke's desire to offend any lingering Victorian proprieties, he also examines Mary's sexual sensations at the moment: "Under her breasts she had / Such multitudinous burnings, to and fro, / And throbs not understood." As she tries to understand what has happened to her, she looks at Gabriel, who is described in terms showing that to Brooke he is the representative of the disembodied love Brooke values so much (and carrying that *fleur du mal* that also marks him as a representative of Brooke's decadent past):

> He knelt unmoved, immortal; with his eyes
> Gazing beyond her, calm to the calm skies;
> Radiant, untroubled in his wisdom, kind.
> His sheaf of lilies stirred not in the wind. (*PW,* 63)

This is not a Christian vision; rather it is Brooke's own personal dream-myth about his relationship with women and his working out of his failure to cross that last barrier between adolescence and maturity: becoming a father. Gabriel is a sexually ambiguous figure who bears close resemblance to descriptions of Brooke: "hair he had, or fire, / Bound back above his ears with golden wire, / Baring the eager marble of his face" (*PW,* 62). As he flies away, "The whole air, singing, bore him up, and higher, / Unswerving, unreluctant. . . . She stood alone" (*PW,* 63). Carnal love has been reduced to a moment of speech—"He told his word" (*PW,* 62)—given by a messenger closer to Apollo than God. Significantly, Brooke carefully selected the same subject for the Eric Gill statues he bought as gifts for both Ka Cox and Cathleen Nesbitt (they may even have been the same statue; a photograph of Nesbitt's is in her memoir): A Madonna and Child.

What may be called Brooke's two political poems are similarly ambivalent. "Seaside" is an early (1908) work; Hassall claims it is his first poem "which could only have been conceived by a natural poet" (Hassall, 151). This sonnet was supposedly inspired by Brooke's decision to sign the Fabian Basis, but no reader without outside biographical knowledge could ascertain this from the poem itself. At a seaside resort (in Brooke's case, Torquay), the speaker finds himself pulled away from the favorably described sensory impressions of people, "the friendly lilt of the band, / The crowd's good laughter, the loved eyes of men," to that ambiguous boundary between nature and humanity, the beach. Out beyond is "The old unquiet ocean." The speaker is suspended, "Waiting for a sign," a phrase emphasized by its placement at the head of the sestet, which although enjambed, is spatially offset. This sign has something to do with the direction of the speaker's life, as he is drawn to the ocean: "And all my tides set seaward." Now the sounds of humanity are not so soothing, as the speaker hears "a gay fragment from some mocking tune." What—or whom does the tune mock? As the tune "dies between the seawall and the sea" (*PW,* 152), the poem ends. Not only is the poem ambivalent about this experience; it is for Brooke uncharacteristically ambiguous. At this point in his life he may have already realized that, although Fabianism held a certain promise for his intellectual visions, it would not lead to any firm personal satisfaction or vocation.

"Second Best," from that same year, is, according to Hassall, Brooke's "only Socialist poem" (Hassall, 117, n.1), yet that becomes apparent only from the imagery near the end of the poem. In it the speaker apostrophizes a heart, probably his own, which he calls "O faithful, O foolish lover." In one of Brooke's favorite settings, outdoors at night, the heart is pondering immortality, and the speaker tells it to "Throw down your dreams," because "night ends all things." Death is final for both joys and sorrows: "That gladness and those tears are over, over," so Death should be greeted "as a friend" (*PW,* 144). Hardened by this realization, the heart is "Exile of immortality" (*PW,* 145). After all this stoic preparation, introduced by the simple conjunction *yet,* comes the image of revolution that Brooke employed in "The Bastille": "Yet, behind the night, / Waits for the great unborn, somewhere afar, / Some white tremendous daybreak." The paradise that will come after this dawn is reminiscent of another of Brooke's Edens, Never Land:

> Ocean a windless level, Earth a lawn
> Spacious and full of sunlit dancing-places,
> And laughter, and music, and, among the flowers,
> The gay child-hearts of men, and the child-faces,
> O heart, in the great dawn! (*PW,* 145)

The lost boys have been found here. This vision also closely resembles the antiseptic, asexual paradise of the Eloi in Wells's *The Time Machine.* Brooke, like many other Edwardians, distrusted optimistic Victorian assumptions about progress; however, how humanity would arrive at this paradisiacal stage with only the help of a poetic image about the day breaking is unclear. One can readily see why Brooke's longer "epic" about socialism proved unworkable.

The path Brooke's politics took toward a more conventional patriotism and idea of order can be seen in what is undoubtedly his most famous (or notorious) poem outside of "The Soldier": "The Old Vicarage, Grantchester." It has inspired extreme reactions from both ends of the political spectrum. For some it is the ideal expression of Georgian bucolics; Denis Cheason has written and illustrated a book about the eponymous house and all the villages and locales mentioned in the poem. For a later socialist like George Orwell, it "is nothing but an enormous gush of 'country' sentiment, a sort of accumulated vomit from a stomach stuffed with place-names"; on its poetic merits it "is something worse than worthless" (Orwell, 1:503). The problem with both views is that they result from not having read the poem carefully enough. One wants to blame Marsh for much of this misreading, since it was he who persuaded Brooke to change its title from "Fragments of a Poem to be entitled 'The Sentimental Exile,'" its title when it was first published in the King's College magazine *Basileon* in June of 1912. Yet even such a clue to the poem's multiple ironies has not prevented a critic from missing its self-deprecating point: "But was it," Alan Read asks, really 'sentimental?'"[8] The answer is that parts of it undoubtedly are, and Brooke's giving it that title is both an admission and an avowal; he will show how such sentimentality can be justified.

Even so harsh a Brooke critic as Samuel Hynes concedes that "Brooke managed in this poem to sustain a tension of attitudes that is missing from his other work" (Hynes 1972, 149). Brooke does this by shifts of tone and perspective that are unusual in his poetry. Most of his poems are short (his favorite form is the sonnet) and strive for and often achieve what Edgar Allen Poe called "totality of effect."[9] "Grantchester" veers around what Bernard Bergonzi has called "a kind of switchback irregularity of tone, alternately satirizing the Cambridge landscape (and by implication the poet) and idealizing it."[10] This "irregularity" would have been much easier for the poem's readers to assess had it kept its original title. Faced with "Grantchester" by itself (or accompanied by at most "The Soldier") in an anthology, readers cannot see that the first lines of the poem—"Just now the lilac is in bloom, / All before my little room" (*PW,* 67)—are, even for Brooke, uncharacteristically fey, self-consciously "Georgian" in the most pejorative sense of the term, and a weakness to which much Georgian poetry, as Brooke well knew, was all too often prone. The speaker is wallowing in a self-indulgent sentimentality. The ellipsis in the first stanza marks the first subtle shift in tone as the speaker wants his desires to be taken more seriously, and the images now begin to recall those of Marvell:

> A tunnel of green gloom, and sleep
> Deeply above; and green and deep
> The stream mysterious glides beneath,
> Green as a dream and deep as death.

Immediately the mood is shattered by the speaker's "—Oh, damn! I know it!" But when he remembers "the day" that "gild[s] gloriously the bare feet," he has slipped into rhetoric again.

The second stanza describes the scene around the Café des Westens in Berlin, where the speaker is recalling the English countryside. It includes the unfortunate but characteristic lines about "*Temperamentvoll* German Jews" (*PW,* 67). Juxtaposed against the disciplined German tulips are the perhaps most successfully realized lines of the poem, as far as its tone is concerned: "Unkempt about those hedges blows / An English unofficial rose" (*PW,* 68). The theme of comfortable English disorganization is continued in the image of "the vague unpunctual star, / A slippered Hesper." It is interesting to note how much Brooke had changed in the year since he'd last visited Germany. He had written to two different correspondents the year before that the Germans were "soft," and to Noel Olivier he explained that, as he was telling the Germans that town life was superior, "Thoughts of English Nature lovers creep into my mind. Oh, it is so easy and so troublesome to love Nature—that way" (*SOL,* 79). Perhaps some of that feeling against oversimplified nature-lovers entered into the third stanza of the poem, when the speaker refers to "clever modern men" in England who "have seen / A Faun a-peeping through the green . . . glimpse a Naiad's reedy head, / Or hear the Goat-foot piping low," a possible veiled reference to the short fiction of another Kingsman, E. M. Forster. The subsequent ellipsis leads to another delicate shift of tone: the lines "flower-lulled in sleepy grass, / Hear the cool lapse of hours pass" (*PW,* 68) are meant to be taken seriously, and the next ellipsis leads into a literary time machine, from which the reader can glimpse Byron ("his ghostly Lordship"), Chaucer, and Tennyson. The feathery satire of these lines leads into the images that so offended Edmund Gosse: a nocturnal vision of "A hundred Vicars down the lawn" and "The sly shade of a rural Dean" who are dispelled by the dawn, "Vanishing with Satanic cries" (*PW*, 69). Brooke could not resist a few more thrusts against religion and refused to remove the offending lines.

The fourth stanza, which begins with the knowingly overhearty "For England's the one land, I know, / Where men with Splendid Hearts may go" (*PW*, 69), contains the beginning of that catalog of place-names which has caused the poem to be both praised and vilified. The humor, or lack of it, in the litany of exaggerated faults of neighboring locales is in the end a matter of personal taste, and a lack of sympathy for Brooke's humor has probably led to the greatest reactions against the poem. The deliberate caricature of the perfection of the place when the speaker again speaks of Grantchester, "A bosky wood, a slumbrous stream, / And little kindly winds that creep / Round twilight corners, half asleep" (*PW*, 70), shows that the speaker is still being self-consciously sentimental. The next lines contain what is perhaps Brooke's last semibalanced view of the Apostles, the gentle humor of

> The men observe the Rules of Thought,
> They love the Good; they worship Truth;
> They laugh uproariously in youth;
> (And when they get to feeling old,
> They up and shoot themselves, I'm told) . . . (*PW*, 71)

This leads into the last and trickiest section of the poem, as far as tone is concerned. Its whole series of questions is a mix of the serious and the ironic. The diction at times approaches the mock-heroic ("ere the night is born") and sometimes is serious and archly overprecious in the same sentence:

> To smell the thrilling-sweet and rotten
> Unforgettable, unforgotten
> River-smell, and hear the breeze
> Sobbing in the little trees. (*PW*, 71)

The realistic description in the word *rotten*, hearkening back to the smell of leaves in "In January," clashes with the pathetic fallacy of the "sobbing" breeze. The questions near the end of the poem come close to the personal anguish that in part prompted the poem, and do not quite fit in with the half-serious, half-flip philosophical questions that precede them:

> Say, is there Beauty yet to find?
> And Certainty? and Quiet kind?
> Deep meadows yet, for to forget
> The lies, the truth, and the pain? (*PW,* 71-72)

Even the use of the dialect phrase "for to" (which functions in Brooke's poetry as a colloquial deflator of rhetoric, as in his poem "It's not going to Happen Again") cannot hide the dropping of the mask in the line referring to all Brooke felt had happened to him—"lies, truth, and pain"—since Lulworth.

Thus, the very last lines of the poem, probably the most well known, assume an air of not what Michael Hastings has called "intolerable smugness"[11] but desperation: "Oh! yet / Stands the Church clock at ten to three? / And is there honey still for tea?" (*PW,* 72). The reader who assumes the poem has only one tone, that of the Georgian version of "emotion recollected in tranquillity," will miss much of the poem's point. Modern readers have been taught that ambiguity in meaning is admirable; ambiguity in tone uncomfortable. The main weakness of "Grantchester" is that the tones are not successfully welded together, and in the last section, the tone is at times impossible to pin down precisely. The problem probably arises because Brooke was essentially an accretive artist; most of his longer works are composed of sections joined together: the chapters in *John Webster and the Elizabethan Dramatists,* the articles that make up *Letters from America.* For all his dreams of being a dramatist, the only play he wrote was one act long. Even some of his longer letters were composed in bits and pieces, a few paragraphs here, some sentences there, over a period of days. As "Grantchester" came to be reprinted, Marsh wanted Brooke to rework it, and Brooke replied, "I fear it's too old for revising. If a couplet or two could be taken out of the last part & shoved in elsewhere, it'd improve the balance. . . . I fear it'll have to remain its misbegotten self" (*L,* 404; ellipsis in original). Brooke dimly perceived that the problem was in that last section, but perhaps if he had attempted to correct the problem the poem would have lost its edge of desperation and have become truly "intolerably smug."

Traveler

Brooke's trip to the South Seas and his stay there were a relatively productive period for him, even though in his letters home he deplored his indolence (he jocularly asked Marsh in his capacity as editor to write a couple of poems for him). The poems that he did write reveal a poet trying to come to some sort of psychic reconciliation with his past. In "It's not going to Happen Again" Brooke has obviously been influenced by the slang and colloquialism he had heard in America and Canada (over which he got into an argument with Marsh, who edited his letters from America before publication). The first stanza of the poem is as full of overblown rhetoric as anything Brooke wrote in his decadent phase: "Like a star I was hurled through the sweet of the world." The second part of the poem collapses this rhetoric with a skilled use of the vernacular in describing those lovers who elsewhere in Brooke's poetry were conventional symbols of passion: "What Paris was tellin' for good-bye to Helen / When he bundled her into the train." The last two lines of the poem, which repeat with studied emphasis the declaration of the title, are addressed not to the "my boy" of the first stanza, Brooke himself, but to an "old girl," probably Noel Olivier (*PW,* 56). The poem "Love" seems to refer to his relationship with Ka Cox, as its lovers are together yet separate, "but taking / Their own poor dreams within their arms, and lying / Each in his lonely night, each with a ghost" (*PW,* 55). In "Mutability" (a favorite poetic subject from Spenser to Shelley), Brooke's Platonism emerges again: "Faith and Good, Wisdom and Truth"—what Brooke calls the *Aeterna Corpora,* eternal bodies, presumably opposed to the physical human bodies doomed to decay—are "subject to no change," unlike human love, in which "The laugh dies with the lips, 'Love' with the lover" (*PW,* 45). One assumes Brooke was referring to this poem when he wrote Marsh from Vancouver, "I contemplate two short Sonnet Sequences (one including *Aeterna Corpora*)" (*L,* 506).

These sonnet sequences were, however, never completed; had Brooke lived long enough to learn to apply himself, the sonnet sequence might have been his best genre, as "1914" indicates. Yet poems with similar themes, and similar attempts at a detached viewpoint, did follow. Death in these poems does not, as it did before in Brooke's poetry, offer a chance to attain a love impossible for beings of flesh; rather, it represents, as it does in his earliest poetry, a rest and surcease from pain. The august but removed beneficence of the "Clouds" becomes a simile for the attitudes of the dead who "remain / Near to the rich heirs of their grief and mirth" and "ride the calm mid-heaven . . . And watch the moon, and the still-raging seas, / And men, coming and going on the earth" (*PW,* 41). The ghostly lover in "Hauntings" is able to remember only "the ecstasy of your quietude," and mainly "Is haunted by strange doubts, evasive dreams, / Hints of a pre-Lethean life, of men, / Stars, rocks, and flesh things unintelligible" (*PW,* 33). In a sense, these are the feelings Brooke had about England and, more particularly, his new upper-class friends, when he was in the South Seas, for he quoted almost identical lines in a letter to Marsh from Tahiti about missing his new circle of friends (*L,* 567).

Several poems from this period reveal the reconciliation Brooke was trying to achieve in his mind about the three main women in his life. "Doubts," originally titled "To Cathleen," is another investigation of the mind-body split; the speaker wonders where his beloved's spirit goes while she sleeps, as she lies "still and fair, / Waiting empty, laid aside, / Like a dress upon a chair." Brooke's old process of idealizing his beloved is fully at work: her soul has "Wings where I may never go." Yet the speaker doubts that her soul really does wander, because her body frowns and smiles as she is asleep. The concluding couplet asks, "And if the spirit be not there, / Why is fragrance in the hair?" (*PW,* 43), thus cleaning up the olfactory image from "Lust" that landed Brooke in a major disagreement with Marsh and Sidgwick—"your remembered smell most agony" (*PW,* 127). This connection of self with smell seems to indicate a tentative coming to terms with the Platonic dualism that had beleaguered him before. And since this dualism had the force of a religion for him, "Doubts" is an appropriate title for the poem. The sense of smell, heretofore associated with sexual desire, is now associated, however tentatively, with the beloved's inner being, as well as her body.

The subject of "A Memory," written in Hawaii, is probably Noel Olivier, and again the speaker confronts his beloved as she sleeps. As the speaker kneels next to her bed, her hand reaches out and unconsciously holds his head, and he "had rest / Unhoped this side of Heaven, beneath your breast." The sestet of the sonnet conflates this moment (which Brooke claimed to Nesbitt actually happened one night) with their whole relationship: "It was great wrong you did me; and for gain / Of that poor moment's kindliness, and ease, / And sleepy mother-comfort!" That last phrase reveals a great deal about what substitutes Brooke was seeking in his relationships with women, a "lap" that he found so comforting and for which he had searched so long. Although admitting all this happens while his beloved sleeps, the speaker cannot help implying a sense of volition to his beloved's actions: the fingers that hold his head are "waking," even if she is not. The conclusion of the poem indicates that in this case the speaker has not yet been able to control his feelings about the past: "And love that's awakened so / Takes all too long to lay asleep again" (*PW,* 39).

According to Hassall, Ka Cox is the subject of "One Day," "Waikiki," and "Retrospect" (Hassall, 416–17, 434). "One Day," however, from what Hassall calls Brooke's "Modern Love" sequence, seems to be more about Noel Olivier. The speaker asserts that he has been happy all day, while he "held the memory of you." He has "sowed the sky with tiny clouds of love" and "crowned your head with fancies . . . Stray buds from that old dust of misery" (*PW,* 38). Poems about Cox rarely admit the *speaker's* love, and the garland of "fancies" fits in more with Brooke's constant image of Noel Olivier as a dryad. The sestet is more ominous; these memories become "a strange shining stone" that a child plays with, ignorant that for its sake "towns were fire of old, / And love has been betrayed, and murder done, / And great kings turned to a little bitter mould" (*PW,* 38). Such a stone is not as "harmless" as Hassall says it is (Hassall, 416), particularly when the poem ends with such images. The transferral of such feelings into the past may be hoped for, but it is not yet complete. The child (another characteristic image) who holds the stone may be unaware of its history, yet the speaker is not. "Waikiki" is more definitely about Cox, and Hassall perceptively points out its similarity to the earlier "Seaside" (Hassall, 417). Again the speaker is at the ocean's edge, but this time it is the music of "an *eukaleli*" that reaches his ears. Now he is not "waiting for a sign," as in the earlier poem, but trying to deal with his memories, and as in "One Day," the memory is objectified and distanced into the dim past and the third person: "I recall, lose grasp, forget again, / And still remember" a story "Of two that loved—or did not love—and one / Whose perplexed heart did evil, foolishly, / A long while since, and by some other sea" (*PW,* 37), words that echo Othello's last speech: "Of one that loved not wisely, but too well; / Of one not easily jealous, but, being wrought, / Perplexed in the extreme" (5.2.344–46). In Othello's case, however, it is easy to discern that he is blaming himself; the speaker in "Waikiki" is indeterminate about who is to blame at the shore of that "other sea," which Hassall identifies as the Starnberger See, where Brooke and Cox once stayed. The use of the adjective *perplexed* would nevertheless seem to indicate that the speaker himself is tentatively ready to accept the blame for the "evil" that had occurred between the lovers.

By its title "Retrospect" reveals the stance Brooke is taking toward his relationship with Cox, although again much of the language in this poem could apply to Noel Olivier as well. Although Hassall bases his identification of the subject of the poem on the use of the phrase "mother-quiet," a similar phrase ("mother-comfort") was used in a poem about Olivier. Perhaps unconsciously Hassall noted the brutality of its line "In your stupidity I found / The sweet hush after a sweet sound" (*PW*, 28), and felt that since Brooke used such phrases in letters about Cox, the poem must have been about her. Brooke, however, was not above calling Olivier stupid as well (Nesbitt seems to be the only woman who escaped such epithets). At any rate, the fact that it is difficult to determine the poem's biographical source indicates that Brooke was coming closer to reconciling and healing his memories for both of his earlier major loves. The speaker declares, in images reminiscent of the nature scenes in "Grantchester," that his "thoughts of you . . . Were green leaves in a darkened chamber, / Were dark clouds in a moonless sky." The speaker's previous use of the word *stupidity* is softened when he remembers his beloved's "vast unconsciousness" (*PW*, 28), which is precisely why he seeks her. The poem, written in Tahiti, cannot help but echo Robert Louis Stevenson's language from "Requiem": "And home at length under the hill!" (*PW*, 29). The beloved's "mother-quiet" will cause "love itself" to "faint and cease," another psychologically revealing line. And in a return to images Brooke employed in "A Memory" and "One Day," the speaker's final wish is to return and lay his head "In your hands, ungarlanded," while he sleeps and she keeps watch over him. There is little doubt that such metaphors, while conciliatory and perhaps therapeutic, are regressive. The speaker returns in imagination to a lover whose motherhood is quiet and whose protection will cause the love in him not to grow but to end.

Many critics have pointed out how Brooke's best poem about his experiences in the South Seas, "Tiare Tahiti," represents a step forward. At its start the poem treats characteristic themes, as the speaker tells his beloved that when they die they will become "dust about the doors of friends, / Or scent a-blowing down the night"; the bodies are no longer for Brooke the habitation of corruption. The paradise they shall enter is Platonic, where "the Eternals are": "The Good, the Lovely, and the True, / And Types," and "instead of lovers, Love shall be; / For hearts, Immutability" (*PW*, 25). In a line that looks forward semiseriously to "The Soldier," the speaker declares that "my laughter, and my pain, / Shall home to the Eternal Brain" (*PW*, 26); so far "Tiare Tahiti" contains few surprises. But in the second long section, the speaker begins to describe how physical objects shall be subsumed into what he has called in the first section "the Eternals": a laugh, feet, hands, braided hair, a head—all connected with the Polynesian names of their owners. He catalogs the visual aspects of nature that will be there as well: the colors of coral, rainbows, birds, sunsets and sunrises. Most important is the figure who will be absent from this scene, the former speaker in Brooke's poetry, who was consumed with the dooms of chronological passion: "one who dreams . . . of crumbling stuff, / Eyes of illusion, mouth that seems, / All time-entangled human love." If all these things subsided into the ideal, the speaker asks, then how can the lovers worship each other? "How shall we wind these wreaths of ours, / Where there are neither heads nor flowers?" (*PW*, 26). Significantly, the speaker here, unlike in "Retrospect," allows his own head to be garlanded as well, because the passion is mutual.

Thus, the last section begins with the command to his beloved to "Crown the hair, and come away!" (*PW*, 27). In a line reminiscent of W. H. Auden's acceptance of mortal frailty in "Lullaby" ("Human on my faithless arm"),[12] the speaker tells Mamua to "Hasten, hand in human hand, / Down the dark, the flowered way." The image of a dark floral place, which before had been separated from the speaker by space ("Grantchester") and time ("Retrospect"), is here accepted and experienced. As Delaney has pointed out, the image of water in "Tiare Tahiti"—its "soft caress"—represents a transformation from its formerly absolutive function in Brooke's poetry (and letters). Its use also shows that the speaker has become one with the world of "The Fish": "Pursuing down the soundless deep / Limbs that gleam and shadowy hair." No longer is there "the strife of limbs"; indeed, the lovers are able to bring the world of color and individuality into the formless depths. The last litany shows that the speaker has embraced what has formerly been mistrusted in Brooke's poetry: "lips that fade, and human laughter, / And faces individual, / Well this side of Paradise!" (*PW*, 27). While this is a crucial progression in Brooke's development, it ultimately proved to be a dead end, for he compartmentalized his experience in the South Seas as rigidly as he did other areas of his life, and he did not live long enough to re-integrate them into his life when he returned to England.

One final poem from this period is significant, since it represents Brooke's response to a criticism that later was to be made often of his poetry: that its language and imagery were too abstract. Marsh wrote to him, "I hope you are writing something objective"; there were too many words like *dear* and *love* in Brooke's recent poems for Marsh's taste (Hassall, 433). In response Brooke wrote "The Great Lover." Its first section is full of the bombast he could produce so unerringly, full of sly echoes of Victorian poetic rhetoric, such as Tennyson's in "Ulysses":

> Shall I not crown them with immortal praise
> Whom I have loved, who have given me, dared with me,
> High secrets, and in darkness knelt to see
> The inerrable godhead of delight? (*PW,* 30)

One cannot parody a style well without being somewhat in sympathy with it, so the catalog of specific sensory images that follows sometimes lapses into a rhetoric of its own, closer to Georgian conventions: "feathery, faery dust . . . And flowers themselves, that sway through sunny hours, / Dreaming of moths that drink them under the moon." Other images in the list smack of Belloc's heartiness: "the strong crust / Of friendly bread; and many-tasting food." Some are familiar from other of Brooke's poems, particularly those images involving smell: "Hair's fragrance, and the musty reek that lingers / About dead leaves and last year's ferns" (*PW,* 31). None of them are overtly sexual. When this litany is complete, the speaker declares, "And these shall pass," and even boasts about their transitoriness: "They'll play deserter, turn with the traitor breath" (*PW,* 32). He claims that he shall awaken in some afterlife but will never be able to reclaim the earthly loves he has listed:

> But the best I've known
> Stays here, and changes, breaks, grows old, is blown
> About the winds of the world, and fades from brains
> Of living men, and dies.
> Nothing remains. (*PW,* 32)

Brooke faintly echoes the verbs of Donne's holy sonnet "Batter My Heart" ("to breake, blowe, burn and make me new"),[13] but while Donne praises God for destroying his personality in order to anneal it, Brooke is now able to exult in ephemerality. The traditional use of the impermanence of the physical world in poetry has been to contrast it to the immortality of art, as in Shakespeare's sonnet 55, "Not marble nor the gilded monuments," and, within that tradition, to immortalize the poet's portrait of his beloved: "So, till the judgment that yourself arise, / You live in this, and dwell in lovers' eyes." In Brooke's terms this Shakespearean vow becomes "that after men / Shall know, and later lovers, far-removed, / Praise you, 'All these were lovely'; say, 'He loved'" (*PW,* 32). In the act of treasuring the most ephemeral objects, Brooke is able to come to terms with what had before most troubled him, the inevitability of changing, growing older, and dying. As he wrote to Keeling in his letter on optimism, "I don't know that 'Progress' is certain. All I know is that change is. . . . All this present overwhelming reality will be as dead and odd and fantastic as crinolines or 'a dish of tay.' Something will be in its place, inevitably. And what that something will be, depends on me" (*L,* 259–60). Unfortunately, Brooke was never able to hold on to such moods consistently.

Soldier

It is almost impossible to disentangle an analysis of Brooke's war poems from the history of their reception, which in many senses mirrors the history of the transformations of attitudes toward the World War I. The poems were immediately grasped at by a wide segment of the public; the issue of *New Numbers* in which they first appeared quickly sold out. Brooke's death ensured that few reading them would be able to separate the poems from the man, and even more so from the myth he had become. When the war became stalemated along the Western front and casualty lists exploded, some began to question the emotions portrayed in Brooke's war poems, while others held on to them for consolation. After the war the poems slowly grew notorious, until their reputation today, when only "The Soldier" is included in anthologies as the archetypal statement of the "old Lie" that Wilfred Owen excoriated later in the war in "Dulce et Decorum Est."

Yet Brooke's war sonnets are the direct outgrowth of the themes and subjects Brooke had been exploring for years. They were not made-to-order propaganda; Brooke had tried and failed to get a job that would make use of any abilities he had in that line. The reality is that the first line of "Peace" ("Now, God be thanked Who matched us with this hour") was true: Brooke's own personal sentiments had been precisely matched with the needs of his time. Nowhere can the transition between personal and public sentiment be more easily seen than in his sonnet "The Treasure," written in August 1914, and meant to be read with the five sonnets of "1914." It is a reverse sonnet, with the sestet preceding the octave. The meaning of the first line, "When colour goes home into the eyes" (*PW*, 24), of which Brooke was inordinately proud, is obscure, but taken with the other five lines it seems to imply the moment of death. Images of sight and sound—"lights that shine," "dancing girls and sweet birds' cries"—are all closed behind an area Brooke is becoming increasingly interested in: "the gateways of the brain." Two symbols of color, "the rainbow and the rose," are also shut by "that no-place that gave them birth." Brooke's refusal to believe in an afterlife has led him to transform utopia into its literal meaning: "no-place," the blankness that precedes and follows life. The mind, which Brooke had heretofore imagined as capable of journeying anywhere, has now shrunk to the limits of the "brain," and the images that "go home" are an amalgam of England (the rose) and the South Seas (dancing girls). When the consciousness dies, so do the perceptions that, the poem strongly suggests, the consciousness has created.

The concluding octave of the sonnet develops the metaphor of "The Great Lover" as a cherisher of images and experiences but in a curious way. The speaker hopes that, before death, time will let him "unpack" his "store" (the alternative title for the poem) in "some golden space," and the poem ends on an extended simile of the memory

> as a mother, who
> Has watched her children all the rich day through,
> Sits, quiet-handed, in the fading light,
> When children sleep, ere night. (*PW*, 24)

Brooke has taken the image of the mother, which is usually applied to various types of beloved women in his poetry, and internalized it into a figure of guardianship and appreciation. It is almost impossible not to be tempted to link this metamorphosis with the feeling he expressed in his letters just before he returned to England ("I've such a warmth for the Ranee" [*L*, 590]), and while Brooke was always temperamentally driven to love more warmly that from which he was absent, he showed an even more intense fondness toward England on his return, an emotion that never abated.

While "The Treasure" might imply some sort of progression in Brooke's development, "Peace," the first of the "1914" sonnets, displays many of the unpleasant characteristics of Brooke's post-Lulworth metamorphosis. The image of the diving swimmer returns in the notorious simile of the recruits (the poem's alternate title was "The Recruit") as "swimmers into cleanness leaping" (*PW,* 19). They are washing away all the evils of modern life, "a world grown old and cold and weary," including what is generally taken to be a kick at Bloomsbury, the "half-men, and their dirty songs and dreary," and a fault that even those who admired and liked Brooke found hard to accept, what he called "all the little emptiness of love!" The war will provide the recruits, whose principal weakness is that they "have known shame," with an opportunity, quite simply, when the rhetoric is stripped away, to die; "the worst friend and enemy is but Death" (*PW,* 19). Thus Brooke has come full circle in his poetry, and the figure of Death that hovers over so much of his early decadent poetry reappears. Most of this would be of interest only to the psychobiographer, did not (as will be shown) so many of Brooke's fellow citizens did share his sentiments that the war represented the chance to flush away all the slackness and foreignness they felt had heretofore sickened and weakened English culture.

"Safety" is addressed to the speaker's beloved and thus narrows the rhetorical focus of the sonnets from the broad "we" of "Peace," specifically the recruits but potentially all of England, to the narrow "we" of two lovers. The "safety" of the poem is, of course, not physical safety but emotional if not spiritual protection. The lovers' safety will be with "all things undying," and in listing them Brooke succumbs to Georgian rhetoric and his own hollow heartiness: "The winds, and morning, tears of men and mirth, / The deep night, and birds singing, and clouds flying, / And sleep, and freedom, and the autumnal earth." There is not one fresh or striking image among them: this is Brooke's "fill-in-the-blanks" method of writing poetry at its most vapid. The sestet once again leads up to death as the ultimate consolation: "And if these poor limbs die, safest of all" (*PW,* 20). It is difficult to believe in the consolatory power of such images, even in a nation in desperate need of them, and while Brooke does allude to death's analgesic effect ("a peace unshaken by pain for ever"), in his own case it provides a cessation not of physical but of mental and emotional pain.

Not surprisingly, sonnets 3 and 4 are both called "The Dead." In both of them the dead are addressed in the third person, with sonnet 3 apostrophizing the bugles that will sound over the dead, and sonnet 4 describing them. The third sonnet contains the notorious simile for the blood that would be spilled in war, "the red / Sweet wine of youth" (*PW,* 21), which provided the title for the worst book written about Brooke. Uncharacteristically, old age is here called "that unhoped serene," but the speaker does define youth's greatest sacrifice: the giving up of the chance to have children, "their immortality," a thought that had been growing in Brooke's own mind as one of the reasons for an urgent wartime marriage. The dead also bring back a series of abstractions— "Holiness," "Love," "Pain," and "Honour," and "Nobleness"—with the ambiguous prepositional phrase "for our dearth," which can mean either that they have come because the English lacked them before the war or that they have come to make up their insufficiency. The last line of the sonnet, "we have come into our heritage" (*PW,* 21) supports the first reading of the phrase, that the war has given the English a chance to fulfill themselves, and continues the theme introduced in "Peace" that the war is a cleansing, revivifying event.

Sonnet 4 returns to the themes of "The Treasure." Those who have died have possessed dawn and sunset "and the colours of the earth," and the rest of the images in the octave follow Brooke's characteristic sensory catalog: "Touched flowers and furs and cheeks" (*PW,* 27). "All this is ended," the octave concludes: Brooke does not say the dead have died, but they have stopped feeling. The sestet is an extended metaphor in which the movements of the sea, a favorite place of contemplation for Brooke, are stilled by "Frost, with a gesture." The description of the frozen sea is by extension a description of the dead: "a white / Unbroken glory, a gathered radiance, / A width, a shining peace" (*PW,* 22). This is the sign Brooke has been waiting for since "The Seaside." Once again a moment has been frozen, but unlike "Dining-Room Tea," in which a moment from life is forever captured, here death itself is embalmed. Peace, a powerful word for those who have suffered the agonies of war, is equally powerful for Brooke, who was ironically searching for peace while waging its opposite.

The last poem, "The Soldier," is Brooke's most famous, the poem inscribed by Eric Gill on his memorial in Rugby chapel, the poem by which Brooke can most easily be identified to people who do not otherwise know his name. Its most famous image, "some corner of a foreign field / That is for ever England" (*PW,* 23), has been exhaustively analyzed and even called a symbol of economic imperialism. More insightfully, the image's origin has been traced to one of Brooke's favorite books, Belloc's *The Four Men,* whose last chapter contains a poem establishing this sentiment: "One with our random fields we grow. . . . He does not die that can bequeath / Some influence to the land he knows . . . He does not die, but still remains / Substantiate with his darling plains."[14] Brooke may have repeated the sentiment, but he vastly improved the rhetoric of the utterance. In an uncanny irony for a poem written in 1911, Belloc's poem also contains an allusion to no-man's land. The use of this phrase by both Belloc and those who fought on the Western front reveals one reason why "The Soldier" became so popular: death had become so anonymous (this war originated the memorials to the unknown soldier), and the struggle for a small piece of territory so seemingly meaningless, that any means that could personalize and localize sacrifice were seized on. The image of the afterlife in "The Soldier" that Dean Inge criticized in his sermon—"a pulse in the eternal mind"—is a continuation of the tentative substitutes for the afterlife that Brooke had been exploring in his recent poetry. Adorned with dreams, laughter, and gentleness, this afterlife is in a sense a regression to the safe and sterile Platonic paradises of Brooke's earlier work. The heaven for which Brooke had been searching so long, now called specifically English, has washed clean the sin and pain of "Peace" ("all evil shed away"), and the "hearts at peace" (*PW,* 23) in the last line of the poem fulfill the promise of the title of the first poem. War, not the political revolution of "The Bastille," will remove guilt and sin.

The fragments Brooke wrote en route to the Dardanelles are curiously ambiguous. While they present certain characteristic images and themes and are thus a continuation of "1914," in several instances they offer hints that Brooke was ready to strike into out what for him would have been new ground and can be viewed as fitting in with various aspects of later English poetry of the war. For instance, in the "Fragment" that Keynes selects to lead off his edition of *The Poetical Works,* the speaker, wandering on deck at night and watching unseen his friends performing various actions, sees all of them in a Platonic simile: "Like coloured shadows, thinner than filmy glass." Then he imagines all of them as dead, "Perishing things and strange ghosts—soon to die / To other ghosts—this one, or that, or I." None of this is unusual for Brooke, but the second stanza of the poem, with its images of masculine beauty and its admission of pity, is strongly reminiscent of the poetry of Wilfred Owen:

> I would have thought of them
> —Heedless, within a week of battle—in pity,
> Pride in their strength and in the weight and firmness
> And link'd beauty of bodies, and pity that
> This gay machine of splendour'ld soon be broken,
> Thought little of, pashed, scattered. . . . (*PW,* 17)

Similarly, "Lines for an Ode-Threnody on England," some of which appropriately was written at 10 Downing Street before Brooke embarked, explores the paradox implicit in "The Treasure": that England, while an external object, is also capable of being completely internalized: "She is with all we have loved and found and known, / Closed in the little nowhere of the brain" (*PW,* 203). Since the poem is in such rough shape, it cannot, of course, bear rigorous analysis; for instance, it has been criticized for the line, of which Brooke was very fond, "In Avons of the heart her rivers run." The objection is that the line amounts to nonsense, because rivers are running in a river. Yet Brooke is working through the double process by which a national entity is created internally by the mind and by which it is extended through sacrifice into "a corner of a foreign field," so perhaps the echolalic metaphor is somehow appropriate.

The other fragments offer few surprises. One recounts how a song from the troop decks reminds the speaker of a memory with his beloved on a hill when "youth was / in our hands" (*PW,* 206). Another connects the present war with the Homeric world: "Death and sleep / Bear many a young Sarpedon home" (*PW,* 205). The last fragment Keynes includes seems like a sequel to "The Soldier," and its last lines are obviously meant by Keynes to be taken as Brooke's epitaph just as much as the earlier sonnet often is: "He is / The silence following great words of peace" (*PW,* 207). Only one fragment indicates any new direction, in which Brooke combines realistic and Georgian diction: "'When Nobby tried . . . To stop a shrapnel with his belly' . . . But *he* went out, did Nobby Clark, / Upon the illimitable dark" (*PW,* 205). This comes closer to the voice and focus of Robert Graves and Siegfried Sassoon. "The Poetry is in the pity,"[15] Owen wrote in the preface to his poems. Whether Brooke could have continued to turn his pity away from the self and toward others is the great unanswered question about the direction that Brooke's war poetry—indeed all of his poetry—would have taken had he lived.

Chapter Three
Brooke's Prose

After Brooke's death some of his friends and acquaintances declared that had he lived, they believed he would have been a greater writer of prose than poetry. For instance, Virginia Woolf wrote that "it might have been in prose and not in poetry that he achieved his best,"[1] but she weakened her argument by claiming that Dryden and Donne were also better prose stylists than poets. To a degree these predictions were based more on faith than evidence. During his lifetime Brooke published no long, sustained piece of prose; his letters from America, for example, had appeared at intervals in the *Westminster Gazette,* and many of his critical pieces were written for Cambridge literary magazines. All of his longer works were published posthumously, to satisfy the hunger for any new work by the war's unofficial laureate. Henry James's last essay, an appreciation of Brooke in all the efflorescence of his late style, was published as a preface to the collected *Letters from America.* Even Brooke's fellowship dissertation, *John Webster and the Elizabethan Drama,* was hauled out for readers during the war. His lurid one-act melodrama, *Lithuania,* however, was not resurrected, perhaps because its brutal plot and theme did not mesh well with his sunny Apollo image (as is the case with Brooke's appreciation of Webster, except that those mordant observations are sandwiched between a lengthy, almost flippant disquisition on the nature of drama and 10 dry and quote-filled appendixes on authorial attributions). *Lithuania* nevertheless was not quite as forgotten as some critics have maintained; Bennett Cerf, for example, included it in a collection of one-act plays in the 1940s. Most of Brooke's other prose, including the important talk on "Democracy and the Arts," was not reprinted until the late 1940s, and many of Brooke's letters not until 20 years after that.

Any judgment of Brooke as a prose writer is therefore much more a case of evaluating an apprenticeship than even a judgment about his poetry is. Perhaps Brooke might have branched out into journalism or the drama had he lived, but any speculation about that must take into account the many unfulfilled opportunities he had to produce journalism, and that for all his declarations about writing plays after *Lithuania,* he produced nothing. Yet when he was polemically motivated, he could come up with an interesting work, such as his representation of his feelings when England declared war, "An Unusual Young Man." More likely, his feud with Bloomsbury and other forms of modernism would have led him to ally himself in some way with Marsh in the rearguard actions that were the later collections of *Georgian Poetry*. While these "what if" speculations about Brooke are almost impossible to avoid entertaining and even more difficult to prove, they do provide a valid insight into the values and methodologies of the critic who makes them.

Letters

For years excerpts from Brooke's letters formed an ineradicable part of most written presentations of the man he was. Edward Marsh, in the interest of supposedly presenting Brooke in his own voice, printed long excerpts from them in his *Memoir*. Similarly, the only interesting parts of the execrable *Sweet Wine of Youth,* the first full-length biography of Brooke, are the excerpts from the letters Arthur Stringer reproduces—none too accurately, unfortunately. For years after Brooke's death, Virginia Woolf and her Hogarth Press tried to publish some of Brooke's letters. In 1936, some 18 years after Marsh's *Memoir,* she wrote to Ka Cox about a plan to publish Brooke's letters to Cox, Dudley Ward, the Raverats, and perhaps Noel Olivier: "He got so much into his letters, judging from the few I have, that they alone would blast Eddy effectively. . . . I can't help feeling that he has been smothered and castrated, and there he is, quite different, and memorable, could we disinter him."[2] Since Woolf also asked Cox if there were "much to be told that isn't in them," Woolf did not realize that an unexpurgated publication of Brooke's letters to those four correspondents would have blasted Brooke much more thoroughly than it would have Marsh.

The next book to depend heavily on the letters was Christopher Hassall's official biography in 1964. This can be confirmed by flipping through the pages and noting the ratio of more densely printed excerpts from the letters to the narrative segments by Hassall. This overreliance resulted from several factors. Hassall died before he was able to correct proofs on the biography, and perhaps given more time, he would have further trimmed the excerpts. Nevertheless, like many other devotees of Brooke, Hassall believed that the letters gave an intimate insight into their author, and the ratio of letters to text might have remained untouched. More important, no edition of the letters had yet appeared, and therefore many of them—particularly the unpleasant series to Cox after the Lulworth debacle—had never been widely read before and certainly seemed to "disinter" Brooke with a vengeance; however, even this supposed frankness had met with opposition from certain of Brooke's friends.

Finally in 1968, some 53 years after their author's death, an edition of Brooke's letters appeared, edited by one of his oldest friends, Geoffrey Keynes. In his preface Keynes explained that part of the reason for their late appearance was a disagreement some 12 years earlier by Brooke's other literary trustees over the propriety of publishing them. They felt Keynes's selection of letters "seriously misrepresented their writer" (L, xi), even though Keynes declared, "As time passed it appeared that I was the only trustee likely to take any active steps towards the protection of Brooke's reputation" (L, x). Keynes eventually came to publish, according to Timothy Rogers's calculation, 574 letters, with some 300 excisions for various reasons.[3] To add to the confusion, Keynes omitted some portions of letters that had appeared in Hassall's biography, and one that even appeared in Stringer's. The editing of the letters sometimes appears to have been almost cavalier. Many of Brooke's friends and his perceptive readers have felt that Brooke's defenders had been protecting a myth by withholding certain evidence about him ever since Marsh's *Memoir*. Even Marsh, whose carefully circumspect *Memoir* was derided by those who knew Brooke when he was alive (Virginia Woolf did so publicly and elegantly in her review of it in *Times Literary Suppplement*), was thought to have gone too far by more fervent protectors of Brooke: as a result, much to his grief Marsh's literary executorship of Brooke was revoked by the terms of Mrs. Brooke's will. Thus, even with the revelations of Keyne's edition of the letters about Brooke's breakdown, his brutal treatment of Ka Cox, and the crude anti-Semitic remarks scattered throughout, many conjectured that the full picture of Rupert Brooke had not yet been presented, and they were correct.

In 1987, to mark the centenary of Brooke's birth (one cannot really say it celebrates it), Paul Delaney published *The Neo-Pagans: Rupert Brooke and the Ordeal of Youth*. Delaney was the first author able to make extensive use of the large collection of material collected in the Brooke Archives at King's College, Cambridge. Delaney printed Brooke's letter to James Strachey recounting, in graphic terms, his homosexual experience with Denham Russell-Smith. Brooke's letters to Ka Cox were even more unsettling than had been apparent from those in Keyne's edition: "'I remember the softness of your body: and your breasts and your thighs and your cunt," he wrote to her; "I really rather believe she's pulled me through. She is stupid enough for me to be lazy and silly enough for me to impose upon her," he wrote at the same time to James Strachey about her (Delaney, 160–61). Many previous suspicions about Brooke were confirmed: the depth of his paranoia, anti-Semitism, homophobia, and antifeminism was as virulent as could be hypothesized from the evidence Keynes had left in the sections of the letters he printed. Delaney's portrait of Brooke, however, was itself slightly skewed to emphasize the prurience of these revelations, understandably so, because they had been hinted at so long.

In 1991 the estate of Noel Olivier finally published most of both sides of the Olivier-Brooke correspondence, with its title aptly chosen from Brooke's poem "The Fish": *Song of Love.* The letters provided no sensational discoveries and often confirmed what had been guessed at before. The Lulworth breakdown was in part precipitated by a crisis in the Brooke-Olivier relationship: Brooke created an ideal Noel Olivier and often castigated the real young woman for not living up to his idealization; Brooke's paranoia, jealousy, and refusal to accept the reality of other people's lives led to the deterioration of their relationship. All of this can be hypothesized from the other letters by Brooke that have been published. What is particularly valuable about this collection, so competently edited by Pippa Harris, Noel Olivier's granddaughter, is that for the first time we can read both sides of a series of letters. Olivier becomes a fascinating figure in her own right as the reader watches her grow from a schoolgirl, shaky in her spelling, commonsensical, aware of her own limitations, into a mature, independent figure who is gently sympathetic to Brooke's vagaries, fantasies, and seemingly perpetual mistaken assumptions about their love. She always seems older than Brooke. He, it seems, never realized that all his "honest" revelations to her about Cox and his later involvement with upper-class society really did hurt Olivier and prevented her from forming any deeper kind of emotion for him. She would not let herself go emotionally until many years later, and then ironically with someone of whom Brooke had been wrongly jealous years earlier: James Strachey.

What picture of Brooke can be gleaned, then, from the piecemeal way in which his letters have been made available? For many it will be a matter of taste. Some of the earlier letters are hard-going. Philip Larkin, a somewhat sympathetic reader, has noted "their determined facetiousness and affectation. . . . It is not so much that one doubts his intelligence or high spirits; it is more his idea of what is funny or charming that puts one off."[4] Undoubtedly, what was so appealing to Brooke's friends and acquaintances in person, and what the letters evoke for them so vividly, is not often communicated to those who never met Brooke in the flesh. His self-admitted habit of posing and masking himself is also off-putting. When Brooke writes to St. John Lucas: "Inscrutable, hideous enigma; old as the Sphinx and thrice as passionless; how are you?" (*L,* 382), and the reader realizes that Brooke at the age of 25 still feels compelled to slip into this costume with such nonchalance, the next 300 or so pages of the *Letters* seem insurmountable. The series of letters to Cox written immediately after Lulworth appear interminable, and since so many of them appear in Hassall's biography, often with a slight difference in editing, a sense of déjà vu is particularly oppressive. Further, any student of Brooke's life must learn to become sensitive to the role Brooke adopts with each correspondent, and glean the truth by comparing the various accounts Brooke makes to each one. And few authors have been as intensely self-aware of their possible place in literary history as Brooke. In 1905 he was writing the man who eventually would edit his letters a half-century later, "But if you are so concerned at the difficulty which will arise when that letter is included in the 'Life and Letters,' you *might* obviate it by dating the letters when you receive them" (*L,* 21). Some eight years later, in the letter to Marsh about why Cathleen Nesbitt was unsuitable as a possible wife—her profession and the "rotten crowd" she associated with—he parenthetically added, "This is the sort of letter that doesn't look well in a Biography," and as Delaney notes in printing this passage, both Hassall and Keynes placated Brooke's shade by omitting it (Delaney, 254, n.7).

Brooke's best letters are often those written to acquaintances, people for whom he did not have to adapt himself or his style: they are vivid, unaffected, and perceptive. His letters to those of his friends like Hugh Dalton and Dudley Ward, who refused to cater to his weaknesses, are enjoyable and often affecting. Virginia Woolf had a high opinion of his letters to her; she could see in them his sympathy as he grew to realize that they shared not only the same doctor but many of the same fears and anxieties. Readers who can accommodate themselves to Brooke's idiosyncrasies will be rewarded with an intensely self-conscious portrait of an often troubled—*self-tortured* would not be too strong a word—poet who failed to realize that his credo of "best of all . . . to *live* poetry" (Hassall, 143) would not be sufficient protection against the pressures of the world and his own personality.

John Webster and the Elizabethan Drama

Had Brooke lived, he might have revised his dissertation before repub-lishing it; then again, had he lived, perhaps few would have wanted to read it. At any rate, *John Webster* remains of interest to the student of Brooke's thought because of its subject matter. Many critics have leapt at the all-too plausible assumption that Brooke's interest in the violent and unbalanced world of Webster's characters, particularly in *The White Devil* and *The Duchess of Malfi,* stemmed from his own psychological crisis and breakdown at Lulworth. Ronald Pearsall declares, "Brooke's real concentration on Webster coincided with his nervous collapse" (Pearsall, 78); John Lehmann similarly finds that "One cannot help feeling that [Brooke's] own emotional upheaval in 1912 deepened his sympathetic response to Webster's obsession with jealousy, ruin and the darkness of fate."[5] It must be noted, however, that Brooke was recommending that his friends read Webster as early as 1906. Other persons have been men-tioned as heightening Brooke's interest in Webster, including Brooke's tutor at Cambridge, Walter Headlam. To connect Brooke's work on Webster too closely with his nervous collapse is to lose sight of the fact that Brooke was artistically as well as temperamentally interested in Webster for a long period and that Brooke worked on the dissertation for a long time both before and after the Lulworth incident; it also neglects the synergy that can be set in motion when an oversensitive personality, under a great deal of pressure, is immersed in such a study. Brooke's interest in Webster was as much a cause as a symptom of his breakdown.

The other reason Brooke's dissertation retains significance is its idio-syncrasy. Academic fashions may have changed in the 80 years since Brooke wrote it, but even so, its willful mixture of tones and presenta-tion, from the provocative Apostolic arguments of the introductory chapters to the dry and factual academic influence-hunting of the 10 appendixes, makes one wonder exactly what King's College was looking for in its fellows. Not every reader has found these gambits engaging. For instance, Christopher Hassall, whom few would accuse of being overly severe about Brooke's writings, has remarked, "we might suspect that in these opening pages one of his principal aims was to weed out his readers by discouraging those of limited patience from reading any fur-ther" (Hassall, 386). It is also difficult to ascertain just how accurate Brooke was in his scholarly judgments. Several later works on Webster

have commented on the liveliness of Brooke's approach, but his main
critical contention in the appendixes seems to have been superseded.

The reader who opens *John Webster and the Elizabethan Drama* and
expects it to discuss its title subjects immediately will be disappointed.
Brooke begins at what for him, with his years of Saturday-night discus-
sions among the Apostles, must have seemed the beginning: his first
chapter, "The Theatre," not only discusses the origins of that genre but
asks the even more basic question, "What is Art?" To confirm the suspicion that an Apostolic air hangs about these investigations, on the second page Brooke is already inquiring about "our states of mind while we
follow these pursuits."[6] The state of mind of the audience becomes
Brooke's touchstone when he examines competing theories of aesthetics:
"But the only way to prove them right or wrong is by introspection into
our states of mind when we hear music or see pictures" (*JW*, 5). Part of
this chapter's discussion of aesthetics was inspired by talks Brooke had
with T. E. Hulme in Berlin. Also, to a certain extent, Brooke is attempting an intellectual as well as a personal break from the influence of the
Apostles, even while he is using their vocabulary. Moore himself was
famous for the precision he required in answers or statements: "Can We
Mean Anything, When We Don't Know What We Mean?" is the title of
one of his papers to the Apostles (Levy, 192). Yet Brooke declares that
such qualifications and definitions are irrelevant: "I am not concerned
with what men may *mean*" (*JW*, 4). All that matters to Brooke are the
effects that the work of art in question produces: "The process of sum-
marising a play thus involves the abstraction of various, more or less
common elements of the successive states of mind the play produces,
and the concocting them [*sic*] into one imagined taste or state of mind,
'the play'" (*JW*, 15). While this may seem to some to be mere intellectual jousting on a distant and forgotten field, no less authorities than C. K.
Ogden and I. A. Richards in their study *The Meaning of Meaning* find
that Brooke here was able "to detect the chink in Professor G. E.
Moore's panoply" by his "lively awareness of linguistic pitfalls"; this
evaluation becomes of further importance when one notes Richards was
one of Moore's students, and maintained that Moore was his greatest
single influence (Levy, 4). Ogden and Richards do, however, concede that
Brooke "does not seem to have considered the matter very deeply, and
had no opportunity of following up the promise of his admirable
approach."[7] Considering Brooke's powers of application, perhaps *inclination* would have been a more accurate term than *opportunity*.

Brooke's second chapter, "The Origins of Elizabethan Drama," is thus almost scuttled from the start, since he admits, "It is absurd to pretend we know . . . what were the people thinking as the waggons rolled by or the actors came out" in medieval or Elizabethan times (*JW,* 27). While conceding that the state of mind produced by the Catholic Mass "is strongly aesthetic" (*JW,* 34), Brooke uses another Apostolic distinction, that between humans used as ends or means, in discussing the nature of religious art, which for him is "an art that, ostensibly educating men to be some way useful, for this life or the next, couldn't help treating them, for a stolen moment, as ends" (*JW,* 30). In his next chapter, "The Elizabethan Drama," Brooke becomes more consciously provocative to general scholarship. He dismisses the entire genre of Elizabethan history plays, including Shakespeare's, because they "preserved the worst features of Elizabethan drama in their worst form; the shapelessness, the puerility, the obvious moralising, the succession scenes that only told a narrative, the entire absence of dramatic unity, the mixture of tragedy and farce that did not come off." Romantic comedies, again not excepting Shakespeare, are similarly rejected: "Neither in themselves, nor as a sign of the taste of the times, have they much value" (*JW,* 58). The only worthwhile genre for Brooke is tragedy, and more specifically, the great tragedies of Shakespeare and Webster from 1600 to 1610.

According to Brooke, much of the writing that took place during this decade, including the love poetry of John Donne, "was alive with passion and the serious stuff of art" (*JW,* 61). In Brooke's eyes this was the golden age of literature in the seventeenth century (and thus his title for the entire work is somewhat misleading, since it does not mention the Jacobean period): "It seemed as though all thought and all the arts at this time became almost incoherent with the strain of an inhuman energy within them, and a Titanic reaching for impossible ends" (*JW,* 62). Brooke notes that scholars before have pointed out the vast differences in quality and type between the literatures of the beginning and end of the seventeenth century. Brooke places the demarcation of the two literatures much earlier: 1611. The reasons Brooke adduces for the tremendous surge in energy in the preceding decade are reminiscent of T. S. Eliot's theory of the dissociation of sensibility. Brooke defines the type of wit that operated in that period with a phrase of Chapman's: it "can make anything of anything" (*JW,* 72). The break that occurred after 1611 happened because "Heart supplanted brain, and senses sense" (*JW,* 72). The triumph of the intellect during this period leads to the figure of

Webster, not only the last of the Elizabethans but "the last of the Earth, looking out over a sea of saccharine" (*JW,* 75). Much of the appeal of authors like Donne and Webster for Brooke lies in their hard, intellectual "realism," as opposed to the "pretty" sentimentality of the later tragicomedians, such as Fletcher; by analogy, the same relationship held in Brooke's mind between his own "unpleasant" poetry and the "dew-dabbling" tendencies of not only many Georgians but much of his own earlier verse. That Brooke felt this analogy in a personal sense can be seen in what seems to be an irrelevant side-attack on critics who find Elizabethan subject matter full of "'gross and vicious realism,'" with "'their pruriency and outspoken uncleanliness of speech'" (*JW,* 85). Brooke reverses these strictures and tars the critics with their own brush: "Anger at this impudent attempt to thrust the filthy and degraded standards of the modern middle-class drawing-room on the clean fineness of the Elizabethans, might be irrelevant in an Essay of this sort" (*JW,* 85–86). This attack is not, of course, irrelevant if one is actually defending like-minded authors such as the Elizabethans against criticisms that have been launched against one's first volume of poems, as happened in Brooke's case with *Poems* in 1911.

Part of this dramatic realism for Brooke lay not only in language and subject matter but also in characterization and motivation. Although Brooke was an early admirer of Ibsen and Shaw, he found characters in modern drama to be too intellectual in continually explaining their motivation: "Characters in a play gain in realism and a mysterious solemnity, if they act unexplainedly on instinct, like people in real life, and not on rational and publicly-stated grounds, like men in some modern plays" (*JW,* 92). Webster and Shakespeare are the supreme tragedians for Brooke because their vision went further and deeper than that of any of their contemporaries. Tourneur, for instance, "could not comprehend those horrors of mind and soul that Shakespeare and Webster knew and Marston glimpsed" (*JW,* 70). These horrors seems to be what drew Brooke to Webster, and, as said before, have led many scholars to forge a link between Webster's and Brooke's psychological interests. Yet most of Brooke's discussion of Webster (which finally begins on page 76 of a 158-page study) deals with other matters. For example, he analyzes Webster's blank verse, finding it "a blank verse for talking rather than reading" (*JW,* 112). He deplores Webster's use of rhyming couplets to end a speech: "It is beyond expression, the feeling of being let down, such couplets give one" (*JW,* 129). He evaluates the effectiveness of the plays' plots and language, declaring *The Duchess of Malfi* better than *The*

White Devil. At one point, he even contradicts the whole thrust of his opening chapters. According to Brooke, "Webster's supreme gift is the blinding revelation of some intense state of mind at a crisis, by some God-given phrase" (*JW,* 100). Nonetheless, he has previously defined his touchstone of dramatic evaluation to be the states of mind of the audience: "A play is good in proportion as the states of mind during the witnessing of it are, in sum, good" (*JW,* 16). Thus, Brooke has to concede, however tangentially, that if one cannot examine the states of mind of the playgoers surrounding the Elizabethan stage, then the critic must analyze the states of mind that are presented by the dramatist in the play itself, not merely the states of mind the play evokes.

Other observations in *John Webster* are significant because of their connections to other writers of Brooke's time. Brooke's metaphor for the relationship of the denotation and connotation of a word is similar to Joseph Conrad's description of Marlowe's storytelling in *Heart of Darkness*—"the meaning of an episode was not inside like a kernel but outside, enveloping the tale which brought it out only as a glow brings out a haze"[8]—or Virginia Woolf's metaphor for life in "Modern Fiction"—"a luminous halo, a semi-transparent envelope surrounding us from the beginning of consciousness to the end."[9] Once again Brooke brings in "states of mind": "A word is an idea with an atmosphere, a hard core with a fringe around it, like an oyster with a beard, or Professor William James' conception of a state of mind. Poets think of the fringes, other people of the core only" (*JW,* 152–53). Brooke also goes into great detail analyzing Webster's use of phrases, ideas, and language he "borrowed" from other writers to use in his plays; he comes to the conclusion that Webster probably kept some kind of a commonplace book beside him while he wrote. Brooke's assessment of this kind of dramatic construction is very much like critical evaluations that have been made of T. S. Eliot's method of writing poetry, particularly *The Waste Land:* Webster's "genius comes out equally in phrases he used to produce far greater effect than they do in the original, by putting them at some exactly suitable climax. . . . [E]very man's brain is filled by thoughts and words of other people's" (*JW,* 146).

Eliot, of course, was also a leader in the critical reevaluation of Webster in the early decades of this century. His most memorable statement about Webster's power, that Webster "saw the skull beneath the skin,"[10] is closely related to the appeal Webster had for Brooke. But even more interesting than Webster's obsession with mortality and morbidity for Brooke was the force with which Webster conveyed his obsession:

"Though the popular conception of him is rather one of immense gloom and perpetual preoccupation with death, his power lies almost more in the intense, sometimes horrible, vigour of some of his scenes, and his uncanny probing to the depths of the heart" (*JW*, 123). For a poet like Brooke, who had proven himself to be more than half in love with the idea of death, such a fixation as Webster's would have been fascinating enough in itself, but according to Brooke, Webster goes beyond that. Near the end of his study, Brooke again attempts to locate the center of Webster's power beyond mere morbidity: "All have noticed his continual brooding over death. He was, more particularly, obsessed by the idea of the violence of the moment of death" (*JW*, 156). Brooke also rejects the pigeon-holing of Webster's drama into the convenient niche of the genre of the revenge-play. For Brooke Webster is sui generis; in effect he is the last tragedian. "Once, in 1624, there was, perhaps, a tragedy of blood, not of sawdust. It is beyond our reach" (*JW*, 116).

If there is any clue to a link between Brooke's work on Webster and his own personal crisis, it occurs on the last page of his study, where he analyzes "the world called Webster." In Brooke's optimistic phases (again, one is sorely attempted to call them manic), he believed in the ultimate free will of human beings. In a revealing letter to Gwen Darwin—it appears to have been composed, as do many letters written during such periods, over a span of days—he revealingly links his belief in free will to his characteristic clean-dirty dichotomy: "External Power? . . . Oh, my Gwen, be clean, be clean! It is a monstrosity. There is no power. Things happen: and we pick our way among them. That is all. . . . But there aren't laws. There aren't. Take my word for it. . . . It wildly enhances one's life when one realizes one's free-will" (*L*, 301–2). If Brooke's crisis at Lulworth made him believe that his own free will was nonexistent, that he himself was a creature impelled by internal and external forces over which he had no control, then it comes out in this last analysis of Webster's view of humanity: "It is inhabited by people driven, like animals, and perhaps like men, only by their instincts, but more blindly and ruinously" (*JW*, 158). In one of the appendixes, Brooke notes, perhaps with some amount of personal affinity, that "the word 'foul' was, characteristically, a common one with Webster" (*JW*, 167), and in these final paragraphs of the dissertation proper Brooke applies it in describing the people in Webster's world. "That is ultimately the most sickly, distressing feature of Webster's characters, their foul and indestructible vitality." They are "foul"—unclean or dirty in Brooke's personal moral language—because they have no control.

Brooke's final portrayal of this moral universe—its language something of a surprise when one remembers this is an academic dissertation—shows that, to a certain degree, the affected poses of his decadent period had become internalized: "Human beings are writhing grubs in an immense night. And the night is without stars or moon. But it has sometimes a certain quietude in its darkness; but not very much"(*JW*, 158). The style and tone of this vision show why Brooke was recommending Webster as early as 1906.

If the Cambridge dons who read Brooke's dissertation were put off by this impressionistic conclusion, then they had the final 10 appendixes—A through J—to assuage their doubts over Brooke's fitness for the fellowship. Revealing in them the uses to which he put the immense amount of reading he did at the Old Vicarage, he attempts to prove, mainly through a scrupulous comparison of language and images, whether or not Webster wrote various plays, what portions of collaborative plays Webster did write, and the dates, sources, and states of the plays Webster undoubtedly did write. While these appendixes are much more academic in their presentation—and thus virtually unreadable and impossible to evaluate unless one is as well read as Brooke in the plays of the period—Brooke does not totally abandon his personal style or method of observation: "In actuality, a good poet or playwright tends to write good and bad things in his own style" (*JW*, 174). One has to wonder, however, whether Brooke could have—or would have—done this sort of writing for the rest of his life. Even though he was elected a fellow on the basis of this dissertation in 1913, he made little effort to take up an academic life before his death. Although he was arranging to go to Cambridge just as the war broke out, it appears as though by merely winning the fellowship he had proven to those who doubted him—his mother, his friends who were still in the academic circle at Cambridge, such as the Cornfords—that he could apply himself and reach such a goal. Its having been accomplished, the goal itself was not much worth doing anything with.

Lithuania

Brooke's only play, *Lithuania,* is deceptively titled, and probably intentionally so, so as to mask its grisly subject matter. Lithuania is merely the country in which the drama is set, and the characters, although given within the play what must have seemed to Brooke appropriately Lithuanian names, such as Ivan and Anna, use British phrases in their speech ("By Jove" and "with her Dad" on the first page, for instance), and thus the play could have been set equally well in, say, Latvia or Estonia, or Grantchester, for that matter.[11] The plot is a macabre reversal of the story of the prodigal son (the parable is alluded to by the vodka-shopkeeper near the end of the play). A stranger (all the characters are referred to by abstractions, such as "the Mother" or "the Vodka-shopkeeper's son," in the dramatis personae and play directions) comes to a hut one night seeking shelter. During conversations with a father, mother, and daughter, the stranger reveals that he is carrying a sizable amount of money. When he goes to sleep, the family plots to kill him. The father, weak and craven, can only do so if drunk, and he leaves to consume the necessary courage. When he does not return quickly enough, the daughter commits the crime. When the father returns, it is revealed that the stranger was actually the family's long-lost son, who had become wealthy and returned to take his family out of their misery and poverty.

As has often been pointed out, this plot is not a new one, and its origins go back to a Welsh ballad, "The Black Monk." Brooke may have been told the story in Berlin by a journalist friend of Dudley Ward as the literal truth. Whatever Brooke's source, his original addition to the tale is the character of the daughter. Critics who have noted this cannot help viewing *Lithuania* in psychological terms. Even Hassall has to admit, "Perhaps in plotting out this savage curtain-raiser at the cafe-table Brooke found some relief, putting to an artificial use one or two corroded pieces of the iron which had entered his soul" (Hassall, 340). Somewhat more bluntly, Pearsall views *Lithuania* as representing Brooke's family "constellation," with the "flatness and automism" of the daughter as representing Ka Cox (Pearsall, 111–12). Such an interpretation, while perhaps psychologically reductive, is strongly supported by the descriptions and actions of the characters in the play, and becomes increasingly convincing when one considers how different *Lithuania* is from anything else in Brooke's writings. The daughter is said to be "just past her youth, . . . squarer [than her mother], heavy-faced and immobile" (*Li,* 361), a physical description that calls to mind that of Cox. The daughter's morals are not overly fastidious; her mother tells her, "A lot of young men smell you out, don't they?" (*Li,* 370). At this point in their relationship, Brooke no longer trusted in Cox's fidelity. The ineffectual father is prone to nervous outbursts, bullied by wife and daughter: "Why do you look at me? What are you both thinking? I don't know what you're thinking" (*Li,* 365).

Similarly, William Parker Brooke was ruled by his wife's decrees and was reported to walk around muttering under his breath, "It is so, all the same" (Hassall, 38). When the father points out that the stranger would be a suitable object for the daughter's attentions, she scornfully replies, using characteristic Brooke language, "He's an undersized, white-handed, dirty little man. . . . He's a little, weak, chattering, half a man: like you" (*Li,* 364). If the stranger is meant to be a stand-in for Brooke, the language, particularly the "half a man," reveals the self-hatred, the fear Brooke had that he himself was one of these creatures, and why the war presented the opportunity for not turning into one of them ("Peace"). Another typical Brooke theme ("Jealousy") emerges when the mother claims that she had many more suitors than her daughter, and the daughter shoots back, "It's a dirty thing to be old and jealous" (*Li,* 367). The character of the son is a cipher, but the manner of his supposed death years ago is significant; he allegedly had met death in the element Brooke so often called cleansing and heal-ing—"He was drowned" (*Li,* 361).

The climax of the play is more Grand Guignol than Abbey Theater, although Brooke, good classicist that he is, has the violence take place offstage. Dress plays a large part in it. The daughter proposes that the mother immobilize the stranger with her skirt: "throw it over him up to the neck and hold it down so as he can't get his hands out. Hold fast" (*Li,* 371). A psychobiographical interpretation of this suggestion is tempting; the mother smothers and immobilizes her child. When the murder actually takes place, it is the daughter rather than the mother who has the requisite courage, and she uses an ax. The mother flees the scene, and when the daughter come in, the mother reproaches her: "You went on and on. I thought you were mad. He cried out his mother, at first" (*Li,* 371). In another bit of macabre humor, the mother observes, "I'll never use that skirt again," and the daughter answers, "You'll never need to" (*Li,* 372). After the grisly recognition scene ("She's got some-thing on her hands, Father!"), all the daughter can say is "They'll put me in prison" (*Li,* 374); she shows no remorse, no love for her brother, no horror for her deed.

Brooke was extremely energetic in trying to get this play performed when he returned to London. He had John Masefield and John Drinkwater read it, and he submitted it to Harley Granville Barker and the Gaiety Theatre in Manchester, among others. The only place it was performed, however, was Chicago, by his new friend there, Maurice Browne, in Browne's Little Theater. Brooke's talents as a publicist were

much more effective in pushing *Georgian Poetry*. One problem with the
play was its brevity; with what would it be performed? Drinkwater,
somewhat surprisingly, suggested it be put on in a music hall. Perhaps
the theme of familial violence has led to the play's being compared, however circumspectly, with the work of the Abbey Theater, particularly *The
Playboy of the Western World* (on a camp-out Brooke himself quoted its line
"and he with the great savagery to kill his Da!" [Hassall, 282]).
Lithuania, however, has little of the power of the Irish plays and on the
whole is not even on the level of other "realistic" dramas that other
Georgian poets were writing (such as Gordon Bottomley's *King Lear's
Wife*), dramas that are themselves largely forgotten today. None of the
characters are interesting; a photograph of Maurice Browne's wife, Ellen
van Volkenberg, playing the daughter is correctly but unappealingly
grim. Brooke's main problem was that perhaps the best producer of such
a work as *Lithuania* was only 12 years old at the time Brooke wrote it:
Alfred Hitchcock.

Criticism

Drama As president of the Marlowe Dramatic Society and would-be
playwright himself, Brooke often wrote about the drama, particularly
the Elizabethan plays being revived at Cambridge (not ones he had anything to do with), as well as two of the most influential dramatists of
the nineteenth century, Ibsen and Strindberg. Many of his ideas are
congruent with the aesthetic he propounded in the early chapters of
John Webster and the Elizabethan Drama. For instance, Shakespeare's
Richard II is for Brooke relatively free of the political lessons that weakened the rest of the plays in the series. Richard himself, a "true artist"
who "finds exquisite aesthetic consolation in the position and emotion
of each moment, regardless of the guilty cause or the fatal outcome"
(*PRB,* 145), is almost a candidate for Moore's Apostles. In a remarkable
observation, considering how often John of Gaunt's speech from
Richard II ("this sceptr'd isle . . . this England") and "The Soldier" have
been used as patriotic clarion calls, Brooke remarks, "And anyhow,
Richard was always more to him [Shakespeare] than England" (*PRB,*
145). While modern audiences, according to Brooke, can never hope to
recapture the feelings of the original audience of *The Knight of the
Burning Pestle,* the play itself is so "lively" that modern audiences lose

little. Its language "plays more directly on your blood than any prose-rhythm has a right to do" (*PRB,* 149).

As far as Ibsen and Strindberg are concerned, Brooke's post-Lulworth prejudices become much more apparent. Whereas he once admired Ibsen, even going so far as to watch performances of Ibsen's plays in Danish in Germany, after Lulworth he complains about "the petulant hermaphrodites Ibsen crowded the theatre with." On the other hand, Strindberg's characters are "far cleaner," and if Strindberg is in fact "filthy," "his is only the transient and tortured filthiness of Delirium," as opposed to Ibsen's "cold and deliberate dirtiness" (*PRB,* 179). One wonders if Brooke is talking about two Scandinavian dramatists or himself and Lytton Strachey. Strindberg is repelled by feminism, which Brooke calls "that denial of sex . . . with its resultant shallowness of women and degradation of man" (*PRB,* 176). Brooke's conclusions about Strindberg's characters are similar to his peroration about "the world called Webster": "By such vast and uncomprehended compulsion are Strindberg's people, in part, moved; as people are in real life, as we are driven, with or against each other, to life or death, to pleasure and pain—but mostly to pain—by forces we can never quite understand, but can agree to deplore" (*PRB,* 179). Brooke admires both Webster and Strindberg as dramatists because they depict a moral universe with which Brooke is psychologically comfortable.

Brooke did little fiction reviewing; he seems to have used the novels of Jane Austen as emotional anodynes. Nonetheless, in a review of Compton Mackenzie's *Carnival* for yet another *Westminster Gazette* competition, he further reveals his own aesthetic and shows himself to be more a modernist in his judgments about fiction than he is usually considered to be. Brooke finds Mackenzie's handling of the relative importance of incidents to be effective: "And always there is a satisfying sense of the inadequateness, the inartistic irrelevance of life. Big events hang on chances. Large issues lead nowhere. The end is only partly connected to the beginning. In the middle of the most important scene rain drives you into a Tube station" (*PRB,* 194). Brooke felt that this was also one of Strindberg's strengths as a dramatic constructionist, particularly in *The Dance of Death* and *The Dream Play;* their example "will assist in breaking down the foolish French-Ibsen tradition of the iron clamps of the 'unities'" (*PRB,* 178). As will be seen, Brooke was a thoroughgoing traditionalist when it came to verse writing, but here he shows himself to be receptive to the modernist and impressionist rebellions against the Victorian conventions concerning unity of action in plot. He also reveals in this review that however much he elsewhere admitted that he adored *Peter Pan* as a play, he had to acknowledge that James Barrie was a sentimentalist.

Poetry   Critics generally agree that the single greatest influence on Brooke's poetry after his decadent phase was John Donne. Hassall, in his introduction to *The Prose of Rupert Brooke,* declares that Brooke "never quite abandoned the master who had rescued him from the late-Victorian 'decadence'" (*PRB,* xl). According to Desmond MacCarthy and Raymond Mortimer, it was Lytton Strachey's interest in Donne that made Brooke study him so closely, but considering that both of Brooke's enthusiastic reviews of Herbert Grierson's edition of Donne's poetry appeared well after the Lulworth crisis, such a connection is unlikely. It is clear that Brooke felt a close personal affinity for Donne's love poetry—he rarely mentions Donne's religious verse—and that several of Donne's poems, especially "The Extasie," provided powerful models for Brooke's later poetry.

Brooke's interest in Donne is part of the larger critical rehabilitation of Donne that occurred in the first decades of this century. For Brooke, Donne's best work appeared in that golden first decade of the sixteenth century (which Brooke in his review of Grierson's edition stretches slightly from 1598 to 1613) which also saw the best work of Shakespeare, Jonson, and, of course, Webster. Brooke declares that the zeitgeist of this era "is almost completely the spirit of Donne" (*PRB,* 86). In defining the kind of wit Donne employed in his poetry, Brooke, as he did in *John Webster,* uses Chapman's couplet: a wit that "can make anything of anything" (*PRB,* 88). But now Brooke is able to elaborate on what such a definition of wit entails: Donne "belonged to an age when men were not afraid to mate their intellects with their emotions" (*PRB,* 88). In Donne are exhibited all the warring components that often troubled Brooke: "He was the one English love-poet who was not afraid to acknowledge that he was composed of body, soul and mind; and who faithfully recorded all the pitched battles . . . of that extraordinary triangular warfare" (*PRB,* 92). The way Donne found relief for this internal struggle was one Brooke often tried to adopt, not always successfully: "He is the most *intellectual* poet in English . . . but when passion shook him, and his being ached for utterance, to relieve the stress, expression came through the intellect" (*PRB,* 94). One other aspect of Donne that Brooke noted, and that can be taken as a personal reference, is his language. "His passionate colloquialism of style has influenced even later poetry" (*PRB,* 91). While Brooke's wide reading sometimes led him to overexhibit his erudition in his diction (*inerrable* and *arval* come immediately to mind), his best poetry is a blend of simple, widely understood words of both Latin and Anglo-Saxon derivation (one poem is even titled "Colloquial").

Another extremely influential poet in England (even more influential than in the land of his birth at this period) was Walt Whitman. Whitman was one of the spiritual progenitors of, among others, Edward Carpenter and the "simple-life" movement, the inheritance of which was all around Brooke, particularly in the neo-pagan circles that emanated from Bedales school and their "dew-dabbling" activities. In a review of Ezra Pound's poetry, Brooke nevertheless called Whitman "a dangerous influence" (*PRB,* 112), mainly because Whitman's poetry resembles prose more than poetry. In matters of form Brooke was a firm traditionalist (much like that American Georgian Robert Frost, whom Brooke would often have run into at Dymock). In notes for a talk to the Fabian Society, Brooke elaborated on his beliefs. Moore's philosophy excused Whitman's poetic formlessness because the states of mind Whitman's poetry elicited were allegedly good; however, for Brooke the most "valuable" states of mind are those evoked by poetry, which Brooke defines as "metre, words, and ideas." Brooke finds meter a universal human longing; "the human creature strives to find rhythm in everything." Therefore, "people who want everyone (or most people) to write like Whitman, are deaf, mad, or wicked" (*PRB,* 173). And even though Whitman is one of the world's great poets, the states of mind that his poetry brings about are not, to Brooke, as "good as all that" (*PRB,* 172). One wonders whether Brooke was here referring to the strong homosexual undercurrents in Whitman's poetry.

Brooke's essay on Robert Browning, originally written for a German magazine, is also interesting for the light it sheds on what Brooke thought most worth saving from the Victorians. He dismisses the usual reasons Browning is both admired and criticized: his obscurity and the alleged "harshness of his metre." According to Brooke, Browning "was one of the greatest masters of metre and of verbal music in the whole list of English poets" (*PRB,* 105). Brooke finds little evidence in contemporary poetry, particularly that collected in *Georgian Poetry,* of Browning's influence; instead, Browning's inheritors are the fiction writers, "who have made the vivid and intimate analysing of various wayward types of the human heart their chief interest" (*PRB,* 107). Brooke claims that

Browning's chief gift to modern poets is his liberation of constraints on setting and language, both of which can now be more realistic and quotidian. Browning made the use of contractions in poetry acceptable, which for Brooke was an important step in freeing poetry from the unnatural limits of conventional Victorian poetic diction. But most of all, Browning was not the novelist manqué or simple moralist some have made him out to be; rather Browning's greatest "claim is that he revealed the infinity of everyday passion and the divinity of ordinary men" (*PRB*, 108). These are themes Brooke himself would have been proud to claim as his underlying tenets.

Brooke's enthusiasm for contemporary verse was more restrained. He reviewed for *Cambridge Review* what he called "great slabs of minor poetry." He wrote to St. John Lucas, with the customary self-deprecation that is one of his most engaging qualities, that "I have read volumes of them, all the same, and all exactly the stuff I write. I frequently wonder whether I have not written several of them myself under a pseudonym, and forgotten about it" (*L*, 77–78). Some of his contemporaries he did admire. When Robert Bridges was made laureate, he wrote Marsh that "I think Yeats worth a hundred of him" (*L*, 404). He wrote a circumspect review of James Elroy Flecker's *Thirty-six Poems,* probably because Flecker was a friend whose vaguely decadent poetic stance Brooke had gone beyond. Brooke's review of Ezra Pound's *Personae* is much more direct. From 1909 until just after Brooke's death, Brooke and Pound both warily circled the other. Both seemed to recognize that they were ambitious; both, to a qualified extent, admired each other. Brooke, however, wrote an article for Harold Monro defending Lascelles Abercrombie from an attack by Pound. As noted before, Brooke deplored Whitman's influence on Pound, especially in matters of form. Brooke explains Pound's employment of free verse as "a youthful protest against the flood of metrical minor verse of today" (*PRB*, 112), a claim that is probably not totally inaccurate. Still, Brooke found Pound's more regular poetry appealing. He concluded that Pound would become memorable when "he turns from prose, admirable prose as it sometimes is, to confine himself to the form in which he wrote *Cameraderie*" (*PRB*, 113). Although Brooke lacked the powers of application to construct a fully developed aesthetic, his reaction to poetic modernism in full bloom—as it was after the war, with its abandonment of traditional poetic forms and its sympathetic antecedents (Webster and Donne)—would have been interesting.

Travel

Letters from America is undoubtedly the most accessible of Brooke's prose works. For John Lehmann it is the evidence that Brooke's future as a writer lay in prose more than poetry. It inspired praise, albeit highly and characteristically qualified, from another seasoned writer about traveling in America, Henry James. Indeed, the book is yet another in a line of works by English writers trying to comprehend exactly what their ancestors had brought about in forming a series of colonies that later became independent (and since Brooke wrote about Canada as well, those which became independent from each other). Peter Conrad has written a book about this whole subgenre of travel literature, *Imagining America,* and discusses Brooke's work in a chapter entitled "Aesthetic America" (and, much to the probable chagrin of Brooke's shade, includes him with Oscar Wilde).[12] While such a general view of Brooke's travel writings is to a certain extent justified—especially the chapters on America, which are admittedly the only ones Conrad considers—taken as a whole, *Letters from America* is a much more personal account. Even though Noel Olivier noted at the time they appeared that the articles betrayed their journalistic origins too openly, and even though Brooke had no chance to revise them for publication (Marsh included Brooke's article on his enlistment in the army, "An Unusual Young Man," as a jarringly incongruous coda to the published volume), *Letters from America* records Brooke's own internal odyssey to "health" as much as it documents the reactions of a young Cambridge Apostle to America in the years immediately preceding World War I.

Brooke is not only an aesthete entering America; he is also a Fabian socialist. He tends, however, to underplay this aspect of his portrayal of America and Canada. After all, he was writing most of them for the *Westminster Gazette,* not the *New Statesman.* For example, at first sight New York seems to Brooke to have an almost religious aura about it, but it is the religion of capitalism: "It had the air, this block of masonry, of edifices built to satisfy some faith, for more than immediate ends" (*LFA,* 7). Later on he reinforces this interpretation, particularly of New York. After describing commercial travelers in his hotel lobby, he remarks, "It all confirms the impression that grows on the visitor to America that Business has developed insensibly into a Religion. . . . It has its ritual and theology, its high places and its jargon, as well as its priests and martyrs" (*LFA,* 26). Yet while Brooke notes this substitution of business for religion, he makes no substantial criticism of American society based on it; it is merely an observation. Similarly, his penchant for realism undercuts his more extravagant descriptions. His ship entering New York harbor is "a goddess entering fairyland"; the whole vista appears "unreal." Then he looks down into the waters of the harbor, and he "knew that New York was a real city. All kinds of refuse went floating by: bits of wood, straw from barges, bottles, boxes, paper, occasionally a dead cat or dog, hideously bladder-like, its four paws stiff and indignant towards heaven" (*LFA*, 8–9). This dead Cerberus guards the gates to paradise. Brooke also uses an allusion to Walter Pater's famous description of the Mona Lisa in *The Renaissance* to both amplify and simultaneously deflate his description of a huge illuminated billboard of a woman's head that winks three times and then disappears: "She is older than the sky-scrapers amongst which she sits; and one, certainly, of her eyelids is a trifle weary. And the only answer to our cries, the only comment upon our cities, is that divine stare, the wink, once, twice, thrice" (*LFA*, 34). Conrad correctly notes that Brooke is fascinated by the whole process of advertising, and claims that it is caused by advertising's resemblance "to his own poetic manner, which is also a hieratic, mystifying species of image worship" (Conrad, 78). Yet Brooke's fascination is at the same time a repulsion against the vacuity of the message and the stolidity of the observers. "Why this theophany . . . is not asked by their incurious devotees" (*LFA*, 32). The visual references to classical and renaissance icons mixed in with the sounds of the rapid transit and street cries point up to Brooke the lack of connection in such a society. These icons are substitutes for a need that no longer seems to exist in America.

America is also the home of Whitman, and in many of his descriptions of American men Brooke reveals that he initially views America with the eyes of a reader of *Leaves of Grass*. A walk through New York's streets prompts the observation that "The American by race walks better than we; more freely, with a taking swing, and almost with grace." Brooke immediately flattens the hyperbole by admitting he does not know if this results from "living in a democracy" or "wearing no braces" (*LFA*, 16). Similarly, Brooke's first description of a typical American male could serve as a description of a frontispiece to "Song of Myself": "Any sculptor, seeking to figure this Republic in stone, must carve, in future, a young man in shirt-sleeves, open-faced, pleasant, and rather vulgar, straw hat on the back of his head, his trousers full and sloppy, his coat over his arm" (*LFA*, 17). Yet at the end of this chapter Brooke amends this typical portrait; in its place he substitutes the figure of a mechanic he sees driving a car. "He was big, well-made, and strong, and he drove the car not wildly, but a little too fast, leaning back rather insolently, conscious of power. . . . [H]e seemed like a Greek god, in a fantastically modern, yet not unworthy way emblemed and incarnate, or like the spirit of Henley's 'Song of Speed'" (*LFA,* 22). Whitman's loafer, a static observer, has given way to a more appealing figure in motion, purposeful, more simply dressed, wearing only yellow overalls. Such a man's "state of mind," conscious of its own power, is for Brooke more reliable than that of the casual Whitman-derived young man.

One theme that obsesses Brooke throughout his travels is that of youth and age. America is by definition younger than Europe, both as country and as landscape, since it has been perceived by Europeans only for a few centuries. This preoccupation with time and its effects emerges in, for instance, Brooke's simile for the typical "upper-class head": "the face of an only child who has been brought up in the company of adults" (*LFA,* 18). In Boston Brooke attends a baseball game, and is entranced more by the crowd than the game, particularly the cheerleading, which "seemed so wonderfully American, in its combination of entire wildness and entire regulation." Suddenly Brooke, who until now has cultivated and been the figurehead for a cult of youth, feels himself to be the representative of a more traditional society: "Completely friendly and befriended as I was, I couldn't help feeling at those moments very alien and very, very old" (*LFA,* 43). The whole experience of Harvard reminds Brooke of his own collegiate experience: Harvard's "charm is so deliciously old in this land, so deliciously young compared with the lovely frowst of Oxford and Cambridge" (*LFA,* 45). One moment of comic relief occurs at the end of the chapter when an 80-year-old man asks Brooke, since he comes from Rugby, whether he knows Matthew Arnold, and Brooke does not have the heart to explain "that, even in Rugby, we had forgiven that brilliant youth his iconoclastic tendencies some time since, and that, as a matter of fact, he had died when I was eight months old" (*LFA,* 46). More ominous reflections arise when Brooke observes the annual Harvard class reunion and wonders whether "English nerves" (one supposes he really means his own) could stand seeing "with such emphatic regularity, one's coevals, changing in figure, and diminishing in number, summer after summer!" (*LFA,* 43–44). Even more premonitory is Brooke's noticing a large gap in the procession of men between the ages of 50 and 60. The reason, of course, is the Civil War. His friend tells him, "Those who were old enough to be conscious of the war had lost a big piece of their lives" (*LFA,* 44).

When Brooke enters Canada, the whole psychic atmosphere of the narrative changes. Whether this was caused by Canada's closer cultural ties to England or by Brooke's greater spatial distance from home, is not clear. His analysis of eastern Canada's ethnic problems could also be a self-diagnosis of his recent condition: "Montreal and Eastern Canada suffer from that kind of ill-health which afflicts men who are cases of 'double personality'—debility and spiritual paralysis" (*LFA,* 53). The farther west Brooke travels, the more disturbed are his emotional interpretations of his visual impressions. For instance, Brooke's "general impression" of Montreal is fairly neutral; the city "consists of banks and churches," although he does mildly criticize its "air of dour prosperity" (*LFA,* 51). When he leaves the city and looks back on it, however, the evening sunset, combined with the smoke from the ships and the city, evoke a description against which even Blake's satanic mills would seem mild in comparison: "The gigantic elevators and other harbor buildings stood mistily in this inferno. . . . It was impossible to decide whether an enormous mass of pitchy and Tartarian gloom was being slowly moulded by diabolic invisible hands into a city, or a city, the desperate and damned abode of a loveless race, was disintegrating into its proper fume and chaos" (*LFA,* 61). Such overreactions lead to the climax of the whole narrative, Brooke's side trip up the Saguenay River. Since most of these descriptions are replicated in letters home, it seems that Brooke was trying to transcribe honestly and openly his reactions to the scenery, and the high, towering cliffs on either side of the Saguenay bring forth in him not only an intense claustrophobia but a fear of awakening monsters. "The whole scene seemed some Stygian imagination of Dante. . . . Our homeless, irrelevant, tiny steamer seemed to hang between two abysms. One became suddenly aware of the miles of dark water beneath. I found that under a prolonged gaze the face of the river began to writhe and eddy, as if from some horrible suppressed emotion. It seemed likely that something might appear. I reflected that if the river failed us, all hope was gone; and that anyhow this region was the abode of devils" (*LFA,* 69). The dead Cerberus Brooke had noted in New York harbor kept out no one, and here he indeed finds himself on the Styx, only it is an inner river, and he does not yet have the resources to plunge into it and emerge healthy. In fact, when the steamer reaches the point where the Saguenay joins the St. Lawrence, Brooke does indulge in his favorite recreational activity; he seems lulled by the feeling that he is at home, because the color and appearance of the sky are "like an English sky." He disrobes, hesitates on the edge, and then dives in. The wisps of the St.

Lawrence that he can feel are comforting, but the flows from the Saguenay overpower their warmth. "The current was unexpectedly strong. I seemed to feel the two-mile-deep body of black water moving against me. And it was cold as death" (*LFA,* 71). He immediately escapes from the river's grip and retreats to the shore. "Rivers (except the Saguenay) are human," Brooke declares (*LFA,* 77). This plunge into water has none of the revivifying effects for Brooke that immersions in Lord Byron's pool near the Old Vicarage have given him. It is a negative baptism: death without the rebirth. He would have to wait until the South Seas to be born again into his flesh.

That Brooke's experience on the Saguenay has not renewed him is immediately apparent in his description of crossing Lake Ontario. In his mind this great placid inland sea becomes unaccountably malignant: "But these monstrous lakes, which ape the ocean, are not proper to fresh water or salt. They have souls, perceptibly, and wicked ones" (*LFA,* 78). Like the Saguenay, water here is linked with death and corruption: "The lake was a terrible dead-silver colour. . . . Its glint was inexplicably sinister and dead, like the glint on glasses worn by a blind man" (*LFA,* 78). The closest literary analogue to Brooke's descriptions of human beings dwarfed within a malefic landscape here and on the Saguenay is those of Joseph Conrad, whom Brooke admired. The steamer that carries Brooke across Lake Ontario is portrayed in language that could have come out "Youth," *Heart of Darkness,* or *Lord Jim:* "Our boat appeared to leave no wake; those strange waters closed up foamlessly behind her. But our black smoke hung, away back on the trail, in a thick, clearly-bounded cloud, becalmed in the hot, windless air, very close over the water, like an evil soul after death that cannot win dissolution" (*LFA,* 78). These are not the pleasantly innocuous words of the ordinary travel writer. They are not even the words of a perceptive novelist, such as Anthony Trollope or Charles Dickens, who travels to America to investigate customs and social mores. They are the words of a writer whose inner conflict is raging behind or underneath them. Readers who picked up these articles looking for a cheery travelogue must have been mystified.

When Brooke finally reaches Toronto after what amounts to a trip to his own underworld, he is almost bereft of words. In a coda to this chapter that must also have baffled his English readers and certainly angered Canadian ones, he sputters, "one must say something—*what* must one say about Toronto? What can one? What has anybody ever said? . . . It is all right" (*LFA,* 83–84). Only when he reaches the great set piece of American and Canadian travel writers, Niagara Falls, does he regain his inspiration. In his first chapter in *Imagining America,* Peter Conrad compares various descriptions of the falls by different spectators. He perceptively points out Brooke's debt to Walter Pater's metaphor for life in Brooke's visual impression of the falls: "Perpetually the eye is on the point of descrying a pattern in this weaving, and perpetually it is cheated by change" (*LFA,* 89). For Brooke, however, this change is a source of both strength and anxiety: humans can change the pattern by their force of free will, and in this flux, as he wrote to Gwen Darwin, "Things happen, and we pick our way among them" (*L,* 300–301). Thus the characteristic word *plunge* (which he used to describe his leap into the Saguenay) heightens Brooke's summation of the total experience of Niagara: "The real secret of the beauty and terror of the Falls is not their height or width, but the feeling of colossal power and of unintelligible disaster caused by the plunge of that vast body of water" (*LFA,* 91). The same indeterminacy lies in his metaphors for the falls and the rapids below them: "Here the inhuman life and strength are spontaneous, active, almost resolute; masculine vigour compared with the passive gigantic power, female, helpless and overwhelming, of the Falls" (*LFA,* 94). Conrad correctly asserts that in employing the metaphor of gender, "Brooke has wished on them his own sexual disquiet . . . and confided to it his own sexual uncertainty" (Conrad, 23). The result of all these unsettling notions in Brooke is almost too pat for the biographical critic; Brooke confesses that he finds himself drawn to those pieties he had so long rebelled against, the Victorian answers for the world's problems: "The Victorian lies very close below the surface in every man. There one can sit and let great cloudy thoughts of destiny and the passage of empires drift through the mind; for such dreams are at home by Niagara" (*LFA,* 95). These were the same thoughts he wrote about in a letter to A. F. Schofield quoted before in Chapter 1, in a somewhat more overtly disingenuous vein, when he called himself "Wordsworth Redivivus. Oh dear! Oh dear!" (*L,* 491). While Brooke was never totally transformed into a Victorian empire-lover, his personality did undergo a significant retrenchment as a result of what one can only call an existential anxiety over the possibilities of his own free will in a world of flux, the necessity of taking the "plunge." When he later described the inescapable fate that awaited all temporal creations, it was with the same emotions that he accorded death in many of his poems: "In such places, one is aware, with an almost insupportable and yet comforting certitude, that both men and nations are hurried onwards to their ruin or ending as inevitably as this dark flood" (*LFA,* 95–96). While Brooke undercuts these reflections by calling them the product of "the platitudinous heart," they are also the product of a metaphysical wit that relishes paradoxical products, since the end product of the tumult of the falls was a state of mind Brooke had sought so assiduously: "peace that the quietest plains or most stable hills can never give" (*LFA, 96*).

After Niagara Brooke's travels were in what were then mostly underpopulated areas in Canada. Some of his observations combine the new Victorian with the old Fabian. He recounts some heroic tales of the Mounties and laments, "The tragedy of the West is that these men have passed"; western Canada is now full of unscrupulous land speculators, mainly from America, who have made it "the foundation for a gigantic national gambling of a most unprofitable and disastrous kind" (*LFA,* 130). These speculators have been "inspired with the national hunger for getting rich quickly without deserving it" (*LFA,* 131). Mixed in with these judgments are unpleasant xenophobic remarks, such as that about the enclaves of immigrants from eastern and southern Europe in western Canada: "There is every sign that these lumps may poison the health of Canada as dangerously as they have that of the United States" (*LFA,* 112). And his chapter on "Indians," while viewing them in characteristic Brooke terms of age and youth, is all too stereotypical: "Boys they were, pugnacious, hunters, loyal, and cruel, older than the merrier children of the South Seas, younger and simpler than the weedy, furtive, acquisitive, youth who may figure our age and type" (*LFA,* 139).

Yet Brooke's most profound reactions to the open spaces and untrammeled vistas of western Canada once more concern time. Some of these observations are intentionally comic; he asserts to some rival boosters of the growth of Edmonton and Calgary, "not without shame, that my own town of Grantchester, having numbered three hundred at the time of Julius Caesar's landing, had risen rapidly to nearly four by Domesday Book, but was now declined to three-fifty. They seemed perplexed and angry" (*LFA,* 129). Beside such faux naif exchanges are more serious and characteristic reflections. For Brooke each new perspective is virgin; it has never been perceived before. "The soul—or the personality—seems to have indefinite room to expand. There is no one else within reach, there never has been anyone; no one else is thinking of the lakes and hills you see before you. They have no tradition, no names even; they are only pools of water and lumps of earth, some day, perhaps to be clothed with loves and memories and the comings and goings of men, but now dumbly waiting their Wordsworth or their Acropolis to give them individuality, and a soul" (*LFA,* 117–18). It is as if things cannot exist until artists, with their nominative capacity conjure them up with the power of time and its experience. The possibilities of such an untouched, unexperienced environment, however, now afford Brooke the opportunity of revivifying himself. "The air is unbreathed, and the earth untrodden. All things share this childlike loveliness, . . . even the brisk touch of the clear water as you dive. . . . Every swimmer knows it. . . . [I]t touches the body continually with freshness, and it seems to be charged with a subtle and unexhausted energy" (*LFA,* 118). In the coda to his Canadian travels, Brooke finds himself in the position he has struggled to reach artistically: on the heights, in the Rockies. He tries to interpret a feeling he has noticed in the more pleasant natural sections of his North American journey, on the St. Lawrence, the Delaware, in California and Manitoba; he calls it "the strangeness" that arises from this being "an empty land." Loving such landscapes "is like embracing a wraith" (*LFA,* 153). Brooke describes the emotions of a "European" faced with this situation, but the emotions are, of course, not European but personal, and here the existential terror of the fresh landscape overshadows its healing powers: "The air is too thin to breathe. [The European] requires haunted woods, and the friendly presence of ghosts. The immaterial soil of England is heavy and fertile with the decaying stuff of past seasons and generations. . . . For his own forests and wild places are wind-swept and empty. That is their charm, and their terror. . . . Look as long as you like upon a cataract of the New World, you shall not see a white arm in the foam. A godless place. And the dead do not return" (*LFA,* 154–55). For Brooke the very scent of decay—"the sad smell of rotten leaves," in his earliest poetry—is necessary to affirm his own existence, his presence in the cycle of life, and, more important, death. The New World is too new; it does not have its own history, compounded out of personal experience. "For it is possible, at a pinch, to do without gods. But one misses the dead" (*LFA,* 156).

Brooke's letter from the South Seas, which Marsh included in the thus inaccurately titled *Letters from America,* is "Some Niggers," the title of which comes from a statement by an American woman (whom Brooke calls a "Suffragist") who, on seeing some Samoans, exclaimed, "Look at those niggers! Whose are they?" (*LFA,* 159). The political slant of this epigram, which comes directly out of that type of British radicalism which delights in noting inconsistencies in evangelical brands of radicalism, indicates that this letter will focus more closely on politics than those previous, which it does. One reason is that it appeared in the more politically oriented *New Statesman*. Brooke does make the necessary obeisances toward the region's paradisiacal reputation: "In the South Seas the Creator seems to have laid Himself out to show what He *can* do" (*LFA*, 160). But much of the letter discusses the German colonial rule of Samoa. Brooke declares that the Germans have governed well, a significant admission because of the rivalry between England and Germany before the war. Since the missionaries there are mostly English, they have been unable to ally themselves closely with the German government. Trade is fair and well regulated. Brooke reveals his Fabian background slightly when he reports that the chief complaint of the English in Samoa about the Germans, that they are "too kind to the natives," is "an admirable testimonial" (*LFA*, 164). Yet the Samoans seem temperamentally to prefer the British. Only near the end of the letter do Brooke's personal feelings about the islands emerge. All the natural beauties of the place, he maintains, will appear to the white man "inexplicably and almost unbearably, a scene his heart has know long ago, and forgotten, and yet always looked for" (*LFA*, 168), another version of Never Land. In the most revealing sentence, Brooke refers to the islands' power to heal the duality that had bedeviled him so long: the white man "soon learns to be his body (and so his true mind), instead of using it as a stupid convenience for his personality, a moment's umbrella against this world" (*LFA*, 167).

Letters from America, although in certain set pieces a solid example of the traditional travel literature about North America that readers had learned to expect from English writers, is simply too idiosyncratic for its time to have been very successful. It suffers from the weakness of every long work Brooke attempted, an unsettling unevenness of tone. A sketch of a typical New York department store is followed by the Paterian meditation on advertisements; a vivid description of skinning a deer leads to a lament for ghosts. Stylistically, the work as a whole does prove, if not Lehmann's claim that Brooke would have developed into a better prose writer than poet, that Brooke could write solid, engaging prose devoid of the affectations that mar so many of his letters. Some 20 years after *Letters from America*, such English writers as Robert Byron, Evelyn Waugh, and Graham Greene would show how travel literature could recount inner as well as outer journeys. Perhaps then, undertaking "the SCHEME" at the Basel train station, Brooke, more self-aware, could have written a more satisfying and more unified travel book.

Politics

The reader who is familiar with Brooke only from his poetry is often surprised to learn that he was so involved in politics, even more so that it was politics of a mildly radical sort. As shown in chapter 2, the political allusions in Brooke's poems (excluding, of course, the war sonnets) are so veiled as to be almost meaningless. The subject of politics also forms a small basis of his prose writings. Even though Brooke introduced himself to the premier of Canada as "English Socialist and writer," *Letters from America* is no *Road to Wigan Pier.* While more ambitious Fabians produced pamphlets seemingly at will, Brooke left no written political tracts. His political activity was always more performance-oriented, involving speeches and talks, such as his caravan tour through rural England in favor of the Webb's reform of the Poor Law, than written. He did, however, produce two important political statements: "Democracy and the Arts," a talk given before the Cambridge Fabians, and "An Unusual Young Man," an article for the *New Statesman* about the start of World War I.

"Democracy and the Arts" is a paper read to the Cambridge University Fabian Society sometime during the first half of 1910. In 1915 Brooke's mother gave Geoffrey Keynes the manuscript of the talk, which was in pencil and apparently hastily written. With the election of a Socialist government in England in 1945, Brooke's subject entered the realm of possibility, so Keynes published the talk as a small volume in 1946. "Democracy and the Arts" is significant because it is the only available source, other than snippets culled from his letters and biography, of Brooke's radical political thought, and as one might expect, it is a highly personal document, at times almost willfully provocative. Nevertheless, at its beginning Brooke concedes that he has named democracy in the title of his talk rather than socialism because the word *socialism* frightens many people of otherwise good intentions, and to speak of the arts "under socialism" would "drop the pink gauze of unreality" over the discussion.[13] Whatever the new system of government is called, it will entail a great deal of collectivization, while somehow guaranteeing at the same time—Brooke is purposefully vague about this— "great liberty and security and independence for each man" (*DA,* 2). Brooke goes on to define what he means by art, and in doing so he reveals that his thinking about the political aspects of art has undergone a transformation.

After reading William Morris's utopian fantasy in 1907, *News from Nowhere,* Brooke became captivated by Morris's arguments. He wrote to his radical uncle, Clement Cotterill, that he had stayed up most of the night reading *News from Nowhere,* "and ever since I've been a devoted admirer of Morris, and a Socialist, and all sorts of things" (Hassall, 147)—that last phrase a characteristic undercutting so that his correspondent should not take him too seriously. Yet he had also told Hugh Dalton that he was not Dalton's type of socialist; "I'm a William Morris sort of Socialist" (Hassall, 146). Brooke's own notes in the novel reveal that Morris's fantasy, in which England returns to its rural roots, the Houses of Parliament become a manure storehouse, and every person an artist as well as an artisan, affected him deeply, but mainly because it was an answer to unbridled Victorian and Edwardian optimism: "how often it consoles me to think of barbarism once more flooding the world, and real feelings and passions, however rudimentary, taking the place of our wretched hypocrisies. . . . I used really to despair once because I thought what the idiots of our day call progress would go on perfecting itself; happily now I know that all that will have a sudden check" (Hassall, 148). Similarly, while he was impressed by his first meeting with H. G. Wells, he soon grew to distrust Wells's idea of progress. Although it has been neglected by most writers about Brooke, somehow during the years between 1907 and this talk in 1910 he grew to distrust Morris's conception of the universality of the arts. To the Cambridge Fabians in "Democracy and the Arts" he said that any revival of crafts, so dear to any follower of Morris, "must come, if at all, through the Trades Unions" (*DA,* 4), a statement that puts Brooke on the cutting edge of Fabian thought as well.[14] Further, Brooke rejects Morris's joining of arts with crafts, since that often leads to the debasement of real art into the mere enjoyment of pastimes and hobbies. The arts matter for "what we get out of them" (one expects but does not find the phrase "state of mind"), not the "pleasure" artists get out of producing them (*DA,* 5). In contrast to Morris (and Ruskin before him), Brooke contends that great art is produced by individuals, not communities: "It is no good going back to the Middle Ages and the great communal art of the Cathedrals and the folk-songs. If you can revive communal art, well and good. But it is a small thing" (*DA,* 5). Brooke also rejects Morris's premise that anyone can—indeed should—produce a work of art: "Morris said, I believe, that all poetry ought to be of the kind a man can make up while he is working at a loom. Much of his own was. That may be why a lot of it is so dull" (DA, 5–6). The idea that recreation time will be consumed in producing art is spurious as well. Art is a vocation, not an avocation: "Better, almost, a literature of blue-books than a literature of belles-lettres" (DA, 6).

Brooke's rejection of Morris was probably caused by Brooke's own experience as a poet and his exposure to the arguments of Moore and the Apostles. This becomes apparent in Brooke's disavowal of the political function of art, what leftists would later call social realism. "Art is not a criticism of life" (DA, 7); while some plays do discuss economic or social problems, this is not their main reason for existence. "Discussion is merely one of the means, not the end, of literary art" (DA, 7), Brooke declares, employing one of Moore's favorite dualities of evaluation, means and end. Brooke's definition of the function of the artist is close to Joseph Conrad's in his preface to "The Nigger of the Narcissus" (and also echoes the language of his letter on optimism to Ben Keeling): "'I saw— I saw,' the artist says, 'a tree against the sky, or a blank wall in the sunlight, and it was so thrilling, so arresting, so particularly itself, that—well really, I must show you! . . . There!'" (DA, 6–7). Brooke's definition of the ultimate goal of art is also Apostolic in its language: "Art, if it cannot make men much better as means, can make them very good as ends" (DA, 8). Indeed, art leads humans from the impermanence of life and time "on to the Eternal Ends" (DA, 8). Thus Brooke argues for not only the art of Milton and Keats under such a future government, whatever it is called, but also his own form of art.

Brooke also rejects the notion that in the future art must appeal to a mass audience. While that would be ideal, he instead argues for what today would be called target audiences: "We need not complain if the Public only means a mass of little publics" (DA, 9). Even though Brooke is only a few decades past the zenith of the popular Victorian novelists, he declares that the time has vanished when all England would read one great author. To those who argue that universal education will produce a mass audience of impeccable artistic taste, Brooke counters that since the best present public school and university education does not produce an audience of art-lovers, one should not expect it to happen universally in the future. Lest he be accused of denigrating lower-class taste, however, Brooke admits "that it is probably rather better" than that of his own class (DA, 11). Moreover, lower-class literature is vital and revivifying; a group of young Cockney poets in London offer "more hope—and more fulfillment" than present practitioners of traditional verse (DA, 13).

No scheme of supporting artists, no system of patronage, whether political or aristocratic, has, according to Brooke, succeeded consistently. In modern economic terms, artists have to create their own publics, and most cannot. Brooke cites evidence that most poets in England do not make even £50 a year from poetry writing, so they have to live on unearned income, as Brooke admits that he himself does. He proposes that central government committees of 30 members, selected by the Crown and perhaps the universities, be established to support artists. Five hundred pounds a year, and 1000 endowments, would be all that is necessary. Brooke adds several subsidiary suggestions: local governments as well as the central government should subsidize artists, and the copyright on works produced should revert to the state, but artists should have the possibility of greater income if their work proves popular. In addition, funding by private groups might be necessary if a major artist arises whose work is "so monstrously blasphemous or indecent" that no official committee will endorse it (*DA,* 26). While Brooke does not have his own work in mind when he proposes this contingency, he must have realized where his own treatment of "realistic" or "unpleasant" subjects would lead others in the next 10 or 20 years.

Brooke's final appeal, while perhaps self-serving, is also prescient. He recognized from his own experience how much could and could not be realized financially from writing poetry, a fact he even acknowledged in the terms of his will, by bequeathing his royalties to fellow poets with families who needed the income. (Ironically, he became after his death one of the few poets of the twentieth century who would become a best-selling author; Phillip Larkin has remarked that he deliberately did not compare Brooke's sales figures against those of Auden and Eliot.) Brooke therefore demands that "a large proportion of our interest" must be accorded "to contemporary art" (*DA,* 27). When readers answer that their tastes are modern, that they do read such authors as Meredith, Ibsen, and Tolstoy, Brooke answers that those writers are all dead. "Beware of the dead," because they will lead readers "to accept standards that are prepared for" them (*DA,* 28). Once again, Brooke's touchstone for artistic validity is the experience of the audience. Even Shakespeare will one day be unknown, because "the recipient" of his art will have changed of necessity. The person who can get the most out of art is "one who shares with the artist the general feeling for ideas and thoughts and outlook of the time" (*DA,* 28). And those critics like William Archer who declare that, when all social problems have been conquered, art will have no valid subjects are mistaken. Art concerns itself with "the emotions of the individual human heart" (*DA*, 31), and as long as "Death and Fools" exist, so will tragedy and comedy (*DA*, 32). Even though it is a talk rather than an article intended for publication, *Democracy and the Arts* rather than *Letters from America* best shows Brooke's possibilities as a prose writer and the scope and range of his thought when he chose to apply it. It vividly yet elegantly presents a complicated argument and displays a forceful coherence of tone otherwise lacking in much of Brooke's prose.

The title of "An Unusual Young Man" is meant to be taken as the reverse. These thoughts of a young man on hearing that what was to be called World War I was declared are intended to be taken as the representative reactions of someone who is described in the text as "a normal, even ordinary man, wholly English" (*LFA*, 173). The circumstances of the narrative—the man is camping with friends in Cornwall—are so close to Brooke's own that even though Brooke resorted to the hoary expedient of transferring them to a "friend," they were intended to be taken autobiographically as well. While Brooke's private feelings about the war became well-known later, on publication of the reminiscences of friends and his correspondence, this article, along with, of course, the war sonnets, is Brooke's public justification of his commitment to the war, one he felt necessary to make in answer to his former friends in Bloomsbury and at Cambridge who were opposed to it—according to Paul Levy, every Apostle near Brooke's age was a conscientious objector during the war (Levy, 262).

The whole essay is an interesting experiment in a stream-of-consciousness narrative, and not the sort of dogmatic assertions one might expect from the author of "1914." The young man's emotions are at first uncertain and strained. He can recall to his mind only images: at first two pages of memories and experiences, which are what the word *Germany* evokes in his mind. Some part of his mind tells him that he has to hate all these memories, "find evil in them" (*LFA*, 176), but he cannot. Trying to imagine killing his former German acquaintances leads to daydreams of heroic "egotism," which lead to other selfish thoughts: he will be deprived of his art, hobbies, friends; his romantic relationship will be different. These lead into another reverie, in which his thoughts keep returning to two periods in his life, "the days after the death of his mother, and the time of his first deep estrangement from one he loved" (*LFA*, 177). Such internal projections are, of course, psychologically significant in Brooke's case. His maternal need and his romances are once again linked, as they are in his poetry, and here he imagines that his mother, against whom he rebelled, has died at the moment he is ready to become reconciled to her and to England. The purpose of this revelation in the essay is to show that the friend makes the connection between the way his mind operated at those times of crisis and the way it does now, running on two levels, with the unconscious portion "half labouring with some profound and unknowable change" (*LFA,* 177). What emerges from these ramblings about mental processes is "the word 'England,'" which "seemed to flash like a line of foam" (*LFA,* 177). Once again the symbol of the ocean joining the land, as it did in "Seaside," stands for a time of crisis and self-discovery.

This epiphany of the word *England* leads to a fantasy about a German raid, which in turn causes further seemingly unconnected associations, in which Brooke comes to the heart of his essay—a new and personal definition of patriotism: "He was immensely surprised to perceive that the actual earth of England held for him a quality which he found in A——, and in a friend's honour, and scarcely anywhere else, a quality which, if he'd ever been sentimental enough to use the words, he'd have called 'holiness.' His astonishment grew as the full flood of 'England' swept over him on from thought to thought" (*LFA,* 178). At this point the friend is in a passive state psychologically, as the idea of England is compared to an ocean that sweeps over him. The first rush is a series of visual impressions of the English landscape: "Grey, uneven little fields, and small, ancient hedges rushed before him, wild flowers, elms and beeches, gentleness, sedate houses of red brick, proudly unassuming, a countryside of rambling hills and friendly copses" (*LFA,* 178). Running in the background of his mind are old melodies, "an intolerable number of them being hymns" (*LFA,* 178). Then comes a series of faces and scenes, balancing the scenes that meant "Germany" for him before. Among the scenes are, not surprisingly, one of "diving into a little rocky pool through which the Teign flows" (*LFA,* 179), perhaps Brooke's most characteristic trope. Most significant among the faces are "the set of a mouth he knew to be his mother's, and A——'s face, and inexplicably, the face of an old man he had once passed in a Warwickshire village" (*LFA,* 179). The emotional resonances being captured here might be better described as matriotism than patriotism. The old man—indeed the whole landscape—are straight out of the mood that produced Brooke's letter to Keeling on optimism, only here the emotions are linked to a concept that Brooke before had usually mocked: "To his great disgust, the most commonplace sentiments found utterance in him. At the same time he was extraordinarily happy" (*LFA,*

179). When the friend walks back to the train, he has one more pair of complementary memories: the German one is from Brooke's experiences in Munich, when he "had seen a clown, a Pierrot, and a Columbine tiptoe delicately round the deserted corner of Theresienstrasse, and vanish into the darkness" (*LFA,* 179). The English memory is much vaguer: "the lights on the pavement in Trafalgar Square" (*LFA,* 179–80). This delicate transcription of emotions is almost totally undercut, however, by Brooke's insertion of a flippant phrase that he was reported to have made to several friends at the time, "'Well, if Armageddon's *on,* I suppose one should be there" (*LFA,* 180), a glib, throwaway line his denigrators would be able to attach much more tightly to him than the more ambivalent process described throughout the rest of the essay. Even more forgotten is the reason Brooke ascribes for this declaration, that the friend "felt vaguely jealous of the young men in Germany and France" (*LFA,* 180). At any rate, the conclusion of the essay returns to the more ambiguous reactions: "He thought often and heavily of Germany. Of England, all the time. He didn't know whether he was glad or sad. It was a new feeling" (*LFA,* 180).

This new feeling would later, under the influence of Brooke's experiences in Belgium, turn into the patriotic feelings embalmed in the war sonnets. But at the beginning of the war, as Barbara Tuchman describes in *The Guns of August,* events seemed to be in the saddle; Europe found itself plunged into a conflict in which the decision-makers appeared powerless to change the course of history. At this point a well-educated and well-traveled young man like Brooke would not be able to fall quickly into the patriotic attitudes and reactions that have so often been ascribed to him. Germans had not yet been transmogrified into the hated Huns; Brooke had yet to experience personally the tragedy of "gallant little Belgium." The idea of having to kill in pitched battle his former German friends was as yet "ridiculous," until he had undergone what he called a "half-conscious agony," the process of "painting out a mass of associations" (*LFA,* 176). Brooke was always a more complex figure than he has been given credit for, and not merely psychopathologically. Cyril Connolly in *Enemies of Promise* criticized Brooke's diction in this essay, claiming, "His equipment is not equal to the strain. . . . 'Little, small, grey, uneven, ancient, sedate, red, rambling, friendly, unassuming'—true escapist Georgian adjectives. They might all be applied to the womb."[15] One wonders what an "ancient, rambling" womb would look like, not to mention the other adjectives. "An Unusual Young Man" is an important document not only in Brooke's personal history, showing how his acceptance of his vocation as a soldier was a deliberate yet uncon-scious overcoming of his emotions, but also in the history of a nation that was gearing itself up for its first major military crisis in a century. It is as significant a record as George Orwell's similar essay on his own reaction to the beginning of the World War II, "My Country Right or Left." The real preface to the war sonnets is not only "The Treasure"; anyone who reads them should also read closely "An Unusual Young Man."

Chapter Four

Brooke's Reputation

The timing of his death assured both Rupert Brooke's canonization and his later demonization. His reputation was forever frozen as the author of, most importantly, "1914," and also "Grantchester." The war sonnets' somber yet enthusiastic embracing of the sacrifice of British youth was at first avidly seized on by both politicians and public. When the magnitude of that sacrifice became all too apparent, a reaction set in against Brooke, sometimes, as will be seen, in the same writer who had before admired him. Ironically, Brooke's most important critical idea—that the effect of works of art as they were first experienced by their contemporary audiences soon becomes unrecoverable—is crucial in the history of his reputation. For instance, it is difficult now to judge the validity of Robert Graves and Laura Riding's assertion in *A Survey of Modernist Poetry* in 1928 that "Rupert Brooke writing at the present moment unconnected with the war idea would be as coldly disregarded as indeed he was before his death on active service, when practically all the poems for which he has since become famous had already appeared."[1] Which works, and by whom? one must ask. Any objective analysis of Brooke's writing became impossible because of the polemics surrounding the politics of his reputation. The moment of Brooke's death also ensured that the literary parlor game of speculating on what Brooke would have developed into, both artistically and personally, would continue for as long as his writings were discussed. In order to analyze Brooke's reputation and his place in literary history objectively, it is necessary to disengage him from the incalculable tragedy that World War I became and that to a surprising extent, he foresaw. Brooke cannot be isolated, neither from the environment nor the tradition he grew out of. He cannot be singled out in anthologies for the one poem for which he has been depicted as an unconscious, vacuous slogan-monger. That element, of course, can never be eliminated from his writings; nor can the unpleasant aspects of his biography be whitened over. If Brooke's basic literary theory is applied to his own works, then of course the "state of mind" aroused in most thinking readers after 1918 by "The Soldier" will not be, by any stretch of the term, "good." Yet this does not invalidate the states of mind evoked by the poem from 1915 through, say, 1916, or for many other readers afterward. The enormity of the effects of World War I in almost every aspect of human behavior, particularly the literary, cannot be allowed to unduly influence Brooke's placing in literary history. In addition to merely asking which direction Brooke's art would have taken had he lived, an objective study of Brooke will attempt to connect the writing that he did accomplish more closely not only to the Georgian tradition he was so much a part of but to the modernist movement that was developing at the same time and to other literary figures during other wars. Rupert Brooke needs not so much to be rescued as reexperienced and reconnected.

Reputation during his Lifetime

Perhaps the most infamous summation of Brooke's reputation during his lifetime was the short verse by his close friend Frances Cornford, the effect of which she later came to regret:

> A young Apollo, golden-haired
> Stands dreaming on the verge of strife,
> Magnificently unprepared
> For the long littleness of life. (Hastings, 18)

Not only Brooke's physical appearance but the charm of his personality (a charm largely obviated in his letters for those who did not know him personally) were an inescapable aspect of his poetic effect. He vowed to "live poetry," and to many of his contemporaries, unaware of the conflicts that raged within him, this is precisely what he seemed to do. Yet since so many of these acquaintances, such as Walter de la Mare and John Drinkwater, wrote about him later with only this imprecise knowledge, and his more intimate friends who did write about him later either believed, like Edward Marsh, that his reputation had to be protected or felt constrained, like Geoffrey Keynes, not to speak the entire truth publicly, this myth of the poet whose appearance and behavior were totally congruent with his poetry became perpetuated. De la Mare, for instance, wrote about Brooke's personality, "Here in laughing, talking actuality was a living witness of what humanity might at arrive at when—well, when we tread the streets of utopia."[2] Drinkwater in his tribute effused, "His brief life, with its inevitable intervals of temperamental unrest, was

happy in disposition and in event. It shone with many gifts other than
the great gift of poetry. Wit, the cleanest kind of chivalry, inflexible sincerity, and dear courtesy that only the sincere man knows, courage and
reverence duly met, intellectual ease and great personal charm and beauty—all these things made his friendship one of the most treasurable
things of his time" (Drinkwater, 273). Such hyperbole almost cried out
for debunking, and when the truths about Brooke's personality delicately hinted at by Drinkwater in the phrase about "temperamental unrest"
were finally revealed and the inevitable reaction against Brooke's personal character set in, the inadequacy of such a personal stance, implicit
in Cornford's poetic summary, to deal with the complexities of modern
life became stressed, equally unfairly. Brooke is probably forever doomed
to remain hostage to the image of him that was constructed while he
lived, mainly by others but also assisted in large part by himself. As he
admitted to Cornford, referring to his meeting Henry James, "Of course
I did the fresh, boyish stunt, and it was a great success" (Hassall, 277).

The critical reception of the only volume of Brooke's poetry that
appeared during his life revolved, as Marsh feared, around the few
"unpleasant" poems Brooke fought so insistently to include. One review
echoed Brooke's own rationale for expanding his subject matter; the
Morning Post's critic complained that Brooke "seems to have been
oppressed by the dread of writing prettily" (Hassall, 535). Reviewers
detected the mostly baleful influence of, variously, Browning, Byron, and
Donne. Perhaps the most perceptive review was by the best poet among
its critics, Edward Thomas. He accurately found Brooke to be "full of
revolt, contempt, self-contempt, and yet arrogance too." He declared
that if readers "live yet a little longer they may see Mr. Rupert Brooke a
poet. He will not be a little one" (Hassall, 538). When the first volume
of *Georgian Poetry* appeared, Brooke considered himself the least popular
of the poets included in it, and much of his efforts at publicizing it were
also self-promoting. Most of the critics who reviewed it, including Henry
Newbolt, noted Donne's influence on Brooke, and perhaps surprisingly
for the current view of Brooke, which emphasizes his sentimentality and
overemotionalism, also stressed his intellectualism. This quality must
have emerged by contrast to the work by other poets in the volume.
Whatever the reason, Brooke was read by his contemporaries quite dif-
ferently from how he is approached today. He was viewed as embodying
the spirit of youthful rebellion and iconoclasm, a throwback to the metaphysical poets, whose choice of subject matter was seen as either willfully obnoxious or adventurously wide-ranging.

After Brooke's death he received accolades—albeit private ones—from what might seem a totally unexpected source, Ezra Pound, with whom he had sparred over the poetry of Lascelles Abercrombie, even though Brooke confessed to Harold Monro that he was "not so fervent an admirer of Abercrombie's as many people" (*L*, 403). Pound published what seemed to many a particularly tasteless dig at Brooke in the second issue of *Blast*, "Our Contemporaries," which appeared several months after Brooke's death, although Pound defended himself by explaining that it had been written well before April 1914. This short squib claims that "the Tahitian princess" climbed a palm tree when Brooke decided to leave Tahiti, "But he returned to this island / And wrote 90 Petrarchan sonnets."[3] In Pound's correspondence after Brooke's death, however, he was generous in his praise: "He was the best of all that Georgian group."[4] Still, Pound felt that Brooke's poetry was weakened by the poetic company he kept: "Brooke got perhaps a certain amount of vivid poetry in life and then went off to associate with literary hen-coops like Lascelles Abercrombie in his writings" (Pound, 64). He then sounded a note that was to run through Brooke criticism for the next 75 years—Brooke was harmed more by those who wanted to praise him than by his detractors: "And for God's sake if there was anything in the man, let us dissociate him from his surviving friends. Something ought to be done to clear him from the strain of having been quoted by Dean Inge" (Pound, 65). Elsewhere he claimed Brooke "was infinitely better than his friends."[5] Pound's reasons for thinking this are not quite clear, and it seems obvious that he and Brooke shared a mutual distaste for the other's choice of poetic forms. Whether it was Brooke's "unpleasant" poems Pound esteemed or his more "intellectual" ones, such as "The Fish" or "Heaven," is unknown; perhaps his admiration was partly based on the wary admiration of one skilled promoter of his own genre of poetry for another.

Another interesting example of a contemporary's reaction to the myth-making about Brooke is that of his much closer friend, Virginia Woolf. It has been suggested that she repressed her realization of Brooke's death, but the evidence for this is slim. She was disgusted by Marsh's *Memoir*, a judgment she could only intimate in her anonymous review of it in the *Times Literary Supplement*. In her diary she noted, "The book is a disgraceful sloppy sentimental rhapsody, leaving Rupert rather tarnished."[6] In writing to Brooke's mother soon after her review appeared, however, she had to be much more circumspect: "Rupert was so great a figure in his friends' eyes that no memoir could possibly be good enough. . . . One couldn't get near to his extraordinary charm and goodness."[7] What she really felt about him at the time was much harsher, as she remarked in her diary about a meeting with James Strachey over her review: "we couldn't say much about Rupert, save that he was jealous, moody, ill-balanced, all of which I knew, but can hardly say in writing" (V. Woolf 1977b, 1:172). Remarks in her diary about Ka Cox throughout the years seem to indicate that Woolf was jealous of Cox's continued affection for Brooke; Cox had devotedly nursed Woolf though one of her bouts of mental illness, as Cox had in a much different way done with Brooke. In 1923 Woolf wrote about Cox and her son Mark Arnold-Foster, "But she was in some way very pathetic about Rupert. How Mrs. Brooke suddenly smiled at Mark as Ka had never seen her smile, exactly like Rupert."[8]

Nevertheless, as time distanced her from her years of acquaintance with Brooke, that period grew warmer in remembrance. In 1925 she noted in her diary, "Walking past the Darwins I noticed the willows; I thought with that growing maternal affection which now comes to me, of myself there; of Rupert; then I went on to Newnham."[9] These emotions might have been triggered by the death of Jacques Raverat several months earlier, and she had written soon after it to Jacques's wife Gwen much more warmly about Brooke: "Rupert was a little mythical to me when he died. . . . I had a private version of him which I stuck to when [Bloomsbury] cried him down, and shall preserve somewhere infinitely far away . . . based on my week at Grantchester, when he was all that could be kind and interesting and substantial and goodhearted" (V. Woolf 1977a, 3:178). During this week occurred one of the most famous anecdotes about Brooke's method of writing poetry, an incident Woolf first revealed in her review of Marsh's *Memoir*. Brooke, who was writing the poem that became known as "Town and Country," asked "what was the brightest thing in nature?" In her review Woolf said it was Brooke who "decid[ed] with a glance round him that the brightest thing was a leaf in the sun"[10] and thus completed a line in his "fill-in-the-blanks" method of writing poetry: "Cloud-like we lean and stare as bright leaves stare" (*PW*, 124). Leonard Woolf, however, in relating this anecdote in the third volume of his autobiography, claims it was Virginia who made the suggestion: "'A leaf with the light on it,' was Virginia's instant reply" (L. Woolf, 19). Yet in 1934 Virginia Woolf noted in her diary, "Certainly bright leaves do glare as Rupert said,"[11] unconsciously amending the verb. No matter who was responsible for the image, the entire incident bespeaks an ease and an intimacy, the interruption of which was among the worst damages of Brooke's post-Lulworth vendetta against Bloomsbury. Leonard Woolf tells of his and Virginia's meeting Brooke on the street early in 1915, and Brooke, although initially unfriendly, soon warmed up, and they all had a pleasant lunch. Brooke's letter to Virginia Woolf about her mental illness, although distanced by his characteristic hyberbole ("What tormented and crucified figures we literary people are!" [*L,* 364]) reveals Brooke's capacity for sympathy, a quality he should have cultivated more. As Woolf said in one of her most perceptive remarks about Brooke and the whole situation between him and Bloomsbury, "And what Rupert never allowed for was that half of them were every bit as lacerated and sceptical and unhappy as he was" (V. Woolf, 3:181).

Rose Macaulay

Most of Brooke's biographers have, naturally enough, concentrated most closely on the history of his own emotional entanglements, unrequited loves, requited affairs, and Platonic relationships. The emotions that another writer felt about Brooke himself have gone largely unnoted in writings about Brooke, understandably so, because Brooke hardly referred to her in his correspondence and was perhaps unconscious of her feelings for him. Rose Macaulay's name appears only twice in Hassall's biography, but according to Macaulay's most recent biographer, Jane Emery, Brooke "stirred her far more deeply than she touched him."[17] Since their correspondence does not exist, Emery deduced this attachment from the various versions of Brooke-like characters in at least five of Macaulay's novels. The Macaulays knew the Brookes from Rugby, and her father, George Macaulay, was the tutor who advised Brooke to give up classics and concentrate on English literature. Because she was six years older, she was an acceptable companion for Brooke when he went up to Cambridge (the only references to her in Brooke's correspondence come in letters to his mother). Like Virginia Stephen, Macaulay was what Emery calls "a perfect asexual comrade" (Emery, 108); in a letter she admitted that she too bathed at Grantchester, although whether nude or not she decorously does not tell her correspondent, a Father Johnson, but she hints at it elsewhere. Many of her novels contain what Emery calls a "characteristic" bathing scene, an activity that seems to have been as symbolically important to her as it was to Brooke. She also participated in *Westminster Gazette* literary contests. Brooke invited her to accompany him and Dudley Ward on their caravan in favor of Poor Law reform, but her father, mindful of social proprieties, refused her permission. When Brooke went to London, Macaulay met him there several times, and her reminiscences of him there provide a fresh glimpse of the figure he wished to present to the world at the time. "I was envious of Rupert," she remembered, "who walked about the streets without a map, often with a plaid rug over his shoulders, as if he was Tennyson, which seemed to me a very good idea and gave him prestige and people turned to look at him as he strolled though Soho with his golden hair and his rug, and I was proud to be with him" (Emery, 129). Emery claims that Brooke did not recommend Macaulay's inclusion in the first volume of *Georgian Poetry,* because of his sexist beliefs about the capabilities of women poets, but the blame accrues more to Marsh, who accepted little if any advice about editorial matters. Macaulay and Virginia Woolf, however, were the only female recipients of the presentation copies of the volume that Brooke requested.

The three most interesting novels by Rose Macaulay that contain characters apparently based in part on Brooke are *The Secret River, Views and Vagabonds,* and *Non-Combatants and Others.* In *The Secret River* the central figure is a young poet, Michael Travis, whom Emery views as a symbol of Macaulay's own uncertain sexuality, since he seems to embody her yearnings to be a poet and also resembles Rupert Brooke: "Wanting to be male and to be a poet, she created Michael Travis as her hero and alter ego; but Michael Travis is also a young male poet like Rupert Brooke, and he is in danger of being entrapped by a woman who is unworthy of him" (Emery, 114); perhaps Macaulay was also sensitive to Brooke's uncertain sexuality. The scenes of Michael bathing in the river and the mystical climax of the book, in which he is united with a rose, which combines Macaulay's name with Dante's symbol at the climax of *Paradiso,* lead Emery to the conclusion that *"The Secret River* clearly reflects Rose Macaulay's sexual attraction to Rupert Brooke" (Emery, 114). Of course, this tells us much more about Macaulay than it does about Brooke.

Views and Vagabonds, however, affords much greater opportunities for insights into Brooke as he was seen by his contemporaries, particularly his political views. Even though she did not accompany Brooke on his political caravan tour, Macaulay wished to confront his political position, and this novel is the result. Again no character clearly "stands for" Brooke, but many of his political positions are discussed in the context of the novel. The vagabonds of the title are several: Benjamin Bunter, who is almost exactly Brooke's age, is an upper-class young man who forswears his family and becomes an itinerant carpenter (and later, in a reverse recognition scene, happily learns that he is actually lower-class by birth); the Crevequers are itinerant peddlers who become rich through an inheritance and give their money away. Benjamin's brother Jerry is a poet, whose Cambridge rooms are decorated very much like Brooke's in his first year there, but he, unlike Brooke, is completely apolitical and, unlike Brooke, "was no Platonist. And beauty was permanent—the One that remains, while the Many change and pass."[13] Yet he does take Benjie to bathe at Grantchester and have tea at the Orchard. Anne Vickery, who seems to stand for Macaulay's viewpoint, points out that Jerry is "a reasonable, sane young man with a truthful imagination, and sees straight. Poets and artists do. Now Cecil and Benjie aren't poets and artists, but idealists,—theorists. So they can't see the trees for the wood" (Macaulay 1912, 84). Benjamin's tragedy (almost too harsh a term to use in a novel with such a light touch) is that he denies the reality of human beings in order to make them fit with his social scheme. Benjamin's other brother, Hugh, makes the point: "People are so much more important than any cause; they aren't under laws; they make laws" (Macaulay 1912, 39). In this novel Macaulay seems to be calling Brooke back to his best vocation, as a poet, not as a theorist. She also seems to be hinting that a vagabond life such as the Crevequers lead before and after their rich phase is not as bad as Brooke seems to have considered it. At Cambridge Brooke gave a talk to the Carbonari about a book called *The Vagabond in Literature,* in which he said that being a vagabond of the soul meant "a rebellion against the safeties and little confines of our ordinary life" (Hassall, 122–23). In later letters, however, the interior vagabond, that inner rebel, meant to Brooke the selfish part of him; as he wrote to Cathleen Nesbitt, "There are too many vagabond winds blowing through this evil and idle heart of mind, child" (*L,* 571). There is nothing wrong with taking life, it seems Macaulay was saying to Brooke, as the Crevequers do: "to take what arrives and be thankful, to lose all and yet never lose all, because, having nothing, one yet possesses all things" (Macaulay 1912, 281). Emery also finds that *Views and Vagabonds* is Macaulay's answer to Brooke's criticism of organized religion, particularly Anglicanism. Several of the clergymen in the novel are presented positively, as "actualists," including Bob Traherne, a Christian socialist, and the Catholic priest who believes that the church "teaches the folly of leaving the individual out of account, since her mission is to the souls of individuals" (Macaulay 1912, 134). Whatever the lesson in the novel that Macaulay intended for Brooke, his reaction to it will probably never be known, since he was in France recuperating from his breakdown when it was published. The last line of the novel, spoken by Jerry, at any rate sounds like something Brooke would have said in one of his happier moods: "Life is really quite extraordinarily nice" (Macaulay 1912, 308).

Brooke's final "appearance" in Macaulay's fiction comes in a novel written after his death, *Non-Combatants and Others*. After reading Walter de la Mare's eulogy of Brooke, she wrote him a letter of thanks, and as Emery points out, she could not stop using the present tense about Brooke. "My only excuse for writing is that I am so fond of Rupert— we've known each other since we were children—and that I do like your article so much" (Emery, 151). In the novel Basil Doye is a young painter who has been wounded on the Western front and must return to it after recuperating in England. He has been emotionally involved with Alix Sandomir, also a painter, whose physical plainness is contrasted with the attractiveness of her cousin Evie, with whom Basil also becomes involved during the novel. Evie is described in terms that make her physically resemble Brooke's descriptions of Noel Olivier; her general coloring is brown, and she is called a dryad. When Evie and Basil go out, he tells her, "You aren't grown-up enough yet for black coffee, or smoking, or liqueurs. You must meet my mother; you'd learn a lot from her."[14] When Basil thinks about his relationship with Alix, it is in phrases that could have emerged from one of Brooke's letters about relationships before and during the war: "If the war hadn't come just then, he might have become a great deal in love with her. Before the war one had wanted a rather different sort of person, of course, from now; more of a companion, to discuss things with; more of a stimulant, perhaps, and less of a rest" (Macaulay 1916, 73). In a digression about the superiority of the various English shires, especially Cambridgeshire, the narrator says, "The present writer once knew some one who felt it about Warwickshire, but these, probably, are few" (Macaulay 1916, 175); in one of his letters to Lady Eileen Wellesley, Brooke claimed, "I'm a Warwickshire man" and goes on for a paragraph praising it in the mock-epic style of "Grantchester" (*L,* 599). Later on in the same paragraph from *Non-Combatants,* its narrator quotes from "Grantchester" itself. In what Emery accurately calls the climax of the novel, Alix reveals to Basil that she does care for him seriously, as Evie does not, and his answer captures all the accents of Brooke's conversation: "Why, of course—I know. The way you and I care for each other is one of the best things I've got in my life. It lasts, too, when the other sorts of caring go phut" (Macaulay

1916, 135). While Emery notes that "Although the climactic scene may or may not be based on a conversation with Rupert, its emotional conviction shows that Rose understood the pain of unrequited 'fondness'" (Emery, 151), she also cautions that "Rose was 'horrified,' . . . that someone who knew her interpreted the scenes of the novel as autobiographical" (Emery, 152).

There is, however, another level to the importance of *Non-Combatants* in a study of Brooke. The theme of the novel is the confusion that all its characters, including even the wounded soldiers on leave such as Basil, suffer over their roles as noncombatants during this national crisis. As Samuel Hynes shows, the novel is a typical example of the more ambivalent attitudes toward the war in works that were appearing at its midpoint, 1916. The novel also reveals how Macaulay's own attitudes had changed since the beginning of the war. Emery cites one of her poems, "Many Sisters to Many Brothers," as showing that she at first agreed with Brooke's enthusiasm for the war as expressed in "Peace": the poem's female speaker complains that for her, with little to do but knit socks, "a war is poor fun" (Emery, 149), even using Brooke's most notorious description for war's activities, "fun." Yet in *Non-Combatants* Alix's brother reads to her from a book entitled *The Effects of War on Literature:* "The war is putting an end to sordidness and littleness, in literature as in other spheres of human life. . . . We were degenerate, a little, in our literature and in our lives; we have been made great." Of course, the sentiments expressed in that fictional book are exactly those Brooke extols in "Peace": that war is the great opportunity to awaken and escape "from a world grown old and cold and weary" (*PW,* 19). "Who is the liar?" responds Alix, about the author of the book (Macaulay 1916, 44). Macaulay, like so many others, came to realize that those initially enthusiastic beliefs had been ground up in the vast static battles of the war. If Basil Doye is partly modeled on a Rupert Brooke who might have lived until the war's midpoint, which seems possible given the evidence of the text, then *Non-Combatants* is Rose Macaulay's farewell to the optimistic, nonchalant figure that had symbolized the war's hopeful beginnings.[15]

The Great War

Brooke's reputation is so tied up with the attitudes the majority of the British intelligentsia held at various times about the World War I that it is difficult to attain an objective viewpoint. What has often been forgotten is that Brooke's declaration at the beginning of the war sonnets,

"Now, God be thanked Who has matched us with His hour," was true in several senses. Brooke's war poems became so immensely popular because they matched the popular sentiments of a broad range of British society about the war. The avidity with which members of the establishment (and since Dean Inge did so first, it is well to remember that the word *establishment* as a synonym for the power structure was coined by William Cobbett from the *established* Church of England) extolled Brooke's war poems has made the sincerity of their expression forever suspect. As John Lehmann, a sympathetic observer, expresses it, "one can say that Rupert's death . . . was a god-send for the politicians and generals who used him—perhaps without fully realizing what they were doing—to create a legendary inspiration for the national cause, a mouthpiece for patriotic sentiments that demanded simple, exalted expression beyond the ranting of the newspapers and the tub-thumping demagogues" (Lehmann, 150). It was as if Brooke had at last obtained, in a serpentine way, that job he so eagerly sought at the declaration of war, using his intellect to further war aims. Some also see the war as Brooke's way of escaping what for him was the dreadful prospect of growing old. Robert Wohl says, "The war had arrived unexpectedly, like a legacy from an unknown relative, to save Brooke from a fate he had long feared. It provided an escape from the dreary sleep of middle age and conventional living."[16] In this view the war becomes Brooke's Captain Hook, Brooke's chance to proclaim, along with Peter Pan, "To die will be an awfully big adventure."

Nonetheless, a large majority of Brooke's contemporaries totally agreed with the emotions he so effectively summarized in his war sonnets. As Samuel Hynes has said, "There was never a moment of the war after '1914' appeared when Brooke wasn't the most popular war poet, and never a moment when, to the majority of Englishmen, including those in the trenches, his rhetoric did not seem the most appropriate way of speaking and writing about the ideals of war—at least to those back home in England" (Hynes 1992, 109–10). Yet the image of Brooke as a "tub-thumping demagogic" poet who led the sheep of his fellow countrymen to war should be modified. Throughout his life Brooke's stance was a rebel "leader" who was just as much a follower: the decadent rebel against family and school who was a disciple of St. John Lucas; the Fabian rebel who was a disciple of the Webbs; the Apostle who was a disciple of G. E. Moore; the upper-class "Soul" who was a protégé of Edward Marsh. The writer of the war sonnets was rebelling against the intellectuals he had so long consorted with, and as he did so he expressed private emotions that matched popular feelings in language that was entirely personal and characteristic and yet matched images that were also prevalent throughout his culture.

When World War I began, its initial aims and scope were so vague and general that for a long time the war had no "official" name. Many men found their justification for fighting in what reportedly happened later during the invasion and occupation of Belgium, the alleged atrocities that the Germans committed on the Belgian citizenry and that even today are seemingly impossible to verify one way or the other. Brooke himself used the evacuation of Antwerp, which he witnessed, to vindicate his own participation, even though his narratives of that ordeal were not as lurid as the propaganda that was later so vehemently disbelieved by the generation that came of age in the 1920s and 1930s. But in the first months after the declaration of war, apart from the treaty obligations England was fulfilling by its involvement, the real reasons for going to war against Germany seemed almost subliminal. Many of them, however, "matched" the sentiments Brooke expressed in the war sonnets. For instance, British society seemed to be gearing itself for some kind of war—any war—long before the war with Germany began. That war itself, of course, was long foreseen; Brooke had planned to go as a war correspondent for several years before hostilities broke out. Internally, England appeared ready for several possible wars: the British occupation of Ireland threatened civil war; the suffragette movement and its consequent civil disobedience, some violent, threatened a war between the sexes; and the emergence of militant trade unionism to many presaged a war between the classes. In Hynes's analysis, "Rhetorically speaking, [these wars] were already being fought; the language of war had become, by then, the language of public discourse" (Hynes 1992, 7). Brooke was intensely interested in all these possible conflicts: as a Fabian socialist in the class war, as an antifeminist in the suffragette conflicts, and as an Irish sympathizer when from the South Seas he asked his mother to send two guineas in his name for the relief of striking Irish families. Much of England was psychologically primed for some kind of catastrophe.

In the minds of many, England had no one to blame for this state of affairs but itself. England had grown too soft, for a variety of reasons. Some blamed the influence of modernism in the arts; this modernistic tendency was also connected with the decadent movement of the 1890s, which seemingly had been crushed by the Oscar Wilde libel trial. These issues reemerged for many in 1913 when Robert Ross, Wilde's executor, sued Lord Alfred Douglas, the man who was the cause of the original Wilde case, for libel. Brooke himself was interested in the trial but wrote to Ka Cox, by way of not explaining "the whole business," "that's out of your line" (*L,* 439). As Hynes puts it, "England, it seemed, had many enemies, including some at home, and in some English minds those enemies became conflated and confused, so that opposition to one—to modern art or votes for women—came to seem as patriotic as opposition to another, to Germany itself" (Hynes 1992, 10). Brooke himself had written several times, half seriously but nonetheless deliberately, that England had to become a bulwark against Germany and all it stood for: "German culture must never, never, prevail. The Germans are nice, & well-meaning, & they try; but they are SOFT" (*L,* 300). In the same vein Edmund Gosse, a correspondent whom Brooke began to cultivate near the end of his life, wrote in his 1914 essay "War and Literature" that the English "wish for indulgence of every sort," and their "wretched sensitiveness to personal inconvenience" are really "the spectres of national decay," which would be cleansed out by "the sovereign disinfectant" of war (Hynes 1992, 12). These ideas are, of course, similar to the sentiments of the anonymous writer whom Alix calls a "liar" in Macaulay's *Non-Combatants and Others.* Hynes himself quotes the octave of "Peace" and remarks about it, "This is Gosse versified." For Hynes Brooke's war poems "seemed to confront and acknowledge the suffering that war would bring to the nation, and to give that suffering value" (Hynes 1992, 13). Gosse and other critics, however, reached their conclusions based on what they perceived as the overluxuriousness of late Victorian and Edwardian social life, as well as the character-sapping decadent and modernist movements in art. Brooke arrived at his imprecations in "Peace" against "sick hearts that honour could not move" and the "dirty songs and dreary" of "the half-men" from personal experience, reacting against the Stracheys and the rest of the Bloomsbury group (*PW,* 19).

An interesting example of the continuing popularity of Brooke's work during the war is what Vera Brittain has written about them. In her memoirs of the war years, particularly *Testament of Youth,* she provided a record of what the families of those who died in the war suffered. Based on these experiences she became a committed pacifist, who strangely has nothing but praise for Brooke's poetry, particularly the war sonnets, even though she was writing in 1933. She recalls the first time she was introduced to the poems by her tutor at Oxford, and unconsciously echoes Brooke's own aesthetic: "For the young to whom Rupert Brooke's poems are now familiar as classics, it must be impossible to imagine how it felt to hear them for the first time just after they were written. With my grief and anxiety then so new, I found the experience so moving that I should not have sought it had I realised how hard composure would be to maintain." She calls the sonnets "unhackneyed, courageous, and almost shattering in their passionate, relevant idealism," nonetheless, like many others did, she questions the line in "Peace" about "all the little emptiness of love."[17] Would her fiancé, Roland Leighton, she wondered, have those same feelings? Ironically, Leighton did write two lines that echo Brooke's emotions in that poem: in his poem "Ploegsteert" he declares, "I am sickened with Love that lives only for lending, / And all the loathsome pettiness of peace."[18] Yet as Hynes points out, in a letter Leighton wrote in response to Brittain's sending him a copy of the war sonnets, he graphically depicted the carnage in the aftermath of the battle of Loos and bitterly referred to Brooke's metaphor for blood from sonnet 3, "The Dead": "the red / Sweet wine of youth" (Hynes 1992, 112). Nevertheless, Brittain, along with many others like her, continued in her admiration for Brooke's poetry; soon after she received Leighton's letter she quoted from "The Soldier" in her diary, and when another loved one died, she copied into her quotation book Brooke's "Psychical Research" sonnet, with its promise of seeing "no longer blinded by our eyes." Many soldiers as well continued to draw strength from the war sonnets. As Hynes notes, Herbert Read, writing home after going back to the front again, quoted from "Peace" "entirely without irony" (Hynes 1992, 300).

Yet the appalling experience of trench warfare taught Leighton, as it did many others who initially responded enthusiastically to Brooke's verse, that the ideals Brooke lauded in "1914" could not withstand the experiences of 1916. Charles Sorley, another soldier-poet who died during the war, wrote bitterly about what he viewed as the subtext of the war sonnets. He felt Brooke was entirely too selfish, too narcissistic in the emotions he displayed: "He is far too obsessed with his own sacrifice, regarding the going to war of himself (and others) as a highly intense, remarkable and sacrificial exploit, whereas it is merely the conduct demanded of him (and others) by the turn of circumstances, where noncompliance with this demand would have made life intolerable" (Bergonzi, 44). The attitudes of Ivor Gurney, another soldier-poet (who was also a composer), toward Brooke more resemble Leighton's. Immediately after he learned of Brooke's death he wrote favorably about the sonnets but did also in language showing that he was taken more with the sound of Brooke's rhetoric than with the ideas behind them.

"And so Rupert Brooke is dead; still he has left us a legacy of two sonnets which outshine by far any thing yet written on this upheaval. They are as beautiful as music. They are so beautiful that at last one forgets that the words are there and is taken up into ecstasy just as in music."[19] Yet less than two months later he claims, in response to his correspondent's sending him another unnamed sonnet of Brooke, that Brooke was too glib, too facile. "It seems to me that Rupert Brooke would not have improved with age, would not have broadened; his manner has become a mannerism, both in rhythm and diction. I do not like it. This is the kind of work which his older lesser inspiration would have produced. Great poets, great creators are not much influenced by immediate events; those must sink in to the very foundations and be absorbed. Rupert Brooke soaked it in very quickly and gave it out with as great ease" (Gurney, 34). After Gurney had been wounded and gassed during 1916, his reactions toward "1914" became completely reversed, and he wrote a series of poems meant to be read as correctives, "the first Sonnetts [sic] 1917, 5 of them, for admirers of Rupert Brooke. They will make good antitheses" (Gurney, 128). In a letter written a week later, he explained his plan more fully, giving their titles first: "For England. Pain. Homesickness. Servitude, and one other; are intended to be a sort of counterblast against 'Sonnetts 1914,' which were written before the grind of the war and by an officer (or one who would have been an officer). They are the protest of the physical against the exalted spiritual; of the cumulative weight of small facts against the one large. Of informed opinion against uninformed (to put it coarsely and unfairly) and fill a place" (Gurney, 130). Gurney here uses a variation of the military language employed by the vorticists before the war in naming their new magazine: "counterblast." Like Ben Keeling, he betrays the enlisted man's resentment against Brooke's rank and, like many others, criticizes Brooke for not writing from experience; unlike them, however, he admits that such a charge is "unfair." His own war poetry, he admitted, did not have the requisite "devotion of self sacrifice" (Gurney, 178) that the work of Brooke and others trumpeted; his patriotism, though sincere, was of a different sort. Some of that self-sacrificing pose, Gurney, believed, was false, although he conceded, "Brooke was a sincere exception, but then, he was lucky; he died early in the war" (Gurney, 178). And after he learned that Brooke's will had already meant £2000 apiece for his legatees, Gurney ironically observed, "Poetry pays—it took a War to make it; but still, there you are" (Gurney, 232).

Another example of a poet whose attitudes toward Brooke's work became transformed is Wilfred Owen, although the evidence for this is more tangential than in Gurney's case. Some of Owen's early war verse, according to Owen's biographer, Jon Stallworthy, is reminiscent of the war sonnets, and, to Stallworthy, Owen's placing a photograph of Brooke's grave in his copy of *1914 and Other Poems* shows that "he was impressed at least by the legend of the dead poet" (Stallworthy, 140n). Yet the whole body of Owen's later war poetry is a refutation of the sentiments, and above all the language, of Brooke's war sonnets. Although Owen was never as specific as Gurney in his condemnation of Brooke's rhetoric, such a dismissal is implicit in his preface to the volume of poetry that never appeared in his lifetime. His book is not "about deeds, or lands, nor anything about glory, honour, might, majesty, dominion, or power, except War" (Owen, 31). *Love, pain, death,* and *nobleness* are all capitalized by Brooke in his sonnets, but here the only abstraction capitalized by Owen is *war;* it is the only reality. As Hynes says about these later poets of the war, "the truth about war was a matter of language— and especially of the words that you did *not* use" (Hynes 1992, 183).

Two of these poets, however, Robert Graves and Siegfried Sassoon, were almost unwavering in their continued admiration for Brooke, even after their experiences in the trenches. Graves in particular was adamant in professing his respect: "How wrong about Rupert: we all look up to him as to our elder brother and have immense admiration for all his work from any standpoint, especially in his technique on which we all build. I know it is fashionable in some low quarters to pretend to dislike him; but nobody does, really, least of all R. N[ichols], S. S[assoon], or R. G[raves]" (Ross, 266–67, n59). That assertion, however, might have arisen because the correspondent to whom he revealed such esteem was Edward Marsh, who had taken Graves under his wing much as he had done with Brooke, and Graves knew full well what Marsh's attitude would be toward anyone who criticized Brooke. He wrote to Sassoon, probably referring to the previously cited passage from Charles Sorley, "Eddie not quite so sound, because Sorley spoke evil of Brooke in one of his letters, but almost so."[20] He also asked Marsh "not take as offensive" his criticism of Brooke in *Poetic Unreason* (Graves, 157). Another reason for Graves to tread lightly around any mention of Brooke was the fact that Marsh made several gifts to Graves out of what Graves eventually called the "Rupert Brooke Fund." Graves was under the impression that this money came from some proviso of Brooke's will, and he intimated as much in his autobiography, but Marsh quickly disabused him of the notion. Marsh made the grants out of the profits that accrued from his *Memoir* of Brooke. At any rate, Graves, in several of his letters of thanks to Marsh, mentioned that he would be saying "Paternosters" or "Aves" for Brooke's soul. To Robert Nichols, however, perhaps more truthfully, Graves praised Sassoon's poetry, pointing out that it "contains no ode to Kitchener or Rupert Brooke" (Graves, 62).

Yet some of Graves's praise of Brooke to Marsh is free of the tinge of either sycophancy or an embarrassed gratitude. After reading Brooke's *Poems* (and before Brooke's death), Graves exclaimed to Marsh, "What a torture his sensitiveness must always be for him, poor fellow!" (Graves, 30). When Marsh sent him a copy of *Georgian Poetry 1913–1915,* Graves told him that he had loved almost everything in it, "most of all Rupert's 'Heaven' and 'The Great Lover' and 'The Soldier' and all the rest" (Graves, 39). In perhaps the strangest reference to Brooke in all Graves's letters to Marsh, he tells of a curiously Brooke-like dream he had while laid up in a French hospital after being wounded: "This afternoon I had a sort of waking dream about meeting and making friends with Rupert; it was absolutely vivid and I feel now I know him ten times better than before. We talked poetry most of the time and he said, amongst other things, that it wasn't so bad being dead as you got such splendid opportunities of watching what was happening. The thing ended by your Gray's Inn housekeeper appearing, whereupon Rupert went up and had a bath and I saw him no more" (Graves, 56). He wondered to Marsh what had prompted the dream; an amateur analyst might have remarked that it could have been his brush with death, which he relates in the letter with customary British reticent pluck, that moved him to dream of another soldier-poet who died. Graves's subconscious certainly knew enough about Brooke to have Brooke make a characteristic statement about death, and have him perform one of his favorite activities. At an even deeper level, the dream reveals the most significant affinity that poets like Owen, Sassoon, and Graves shared with Brooke. They all thought of themselves as the true Georgian poets, the makers and preservers of the best Georgian tradition, what Graves called in another letter to Marsh "the excellent Abercrombie-Hodgson-de la Mare-Davies-Brooke tradition of early Georgianism," in contrast to the "sham-Georgian school" (Graves, 136), a school whose weakness and overprettiness would eventually come to blacken all Georgian poetry. As Hynes has shown, one of the gulfs the war established was between the poets who fought and those who did not; poets like Graves and Sassoon "were the real Lost Generation, not the men who died; they had fallen out of the literary world of their own time, into the gap of the war" (Hynes 1992, 339), as modernism became more and more established as the leading poetic movement. Graves might have hidden some of his distaste for the rhetoric of the war sonnets from Marsh, but much of his admiration for Brooke's achievement and method was real; that was the underlying meaning of Brooke and Graves talking about poetry during that hospital reverie.

The fact of Brooke's death, its timing and manner, has been a large part of the myth-making about him and the later controversy over his reputation. D. H. Lawrence's remark in a letter to Ottoline Morrell reveals not only his characteristic hyperbole but that to a certain extent he shared the sentiments of Frances Cornford's verse: Brooke "was slain by bright Phoebus' shaft—it was in keeping with his general sunniness—it was the real climax of his pose. I first heard of him as a Greek god under a Japanese sunshade, reading poetry at Grantchester. . . . Bright Phoebus smote him down. It is all in the saga."[21] Lawrence also understood that this legend-building fit in with Brooke's conscious adoption of an image—"his pose." In a similar vein, Graves told Marsh that "my Father (dear old man!) said that this was a fitting end for Rupert, killed by the arrows of the jealous Musagetes in his own Greek islands" (Graves, 31). As a capstone to all this mythification, Brooke himself anticipated it in a letter to Abercrombie about his attack of sunstroke in Egypt: "The Sun God, (he, the Song God) distinguished one of his most dangerous rivals since Marsyas. . . . He unslung his bow" (*L*, 677). Although Brooke's metaphor was meant to be taken humorously, the reaction against the other overstatements was predictably harsh. Many pointed out that Brooke did not even die in combat; his death was variously attributed to infection from a mosquito bite or a scorpion sting, and Noel Olivier was even questioned in her capacity as doctor as to whether Brooke could have died from complications from a venereal disease. A countermyth grew in which Brooke was a soldier who did not even participate in combat. Hynes, in an essay on Brooke, echoes Sorley's charges and ignores Brooke's experience under fire at Antwerp: "Poor Brooke never got past the self-glorifying stage, because he did not get to the war" (Hynes 1972, 145). Robert Wohl, in his otherwise excellent study of the entire European generation that fought during World War I, makes a fine distinction that readers unfamiliar with Brooke's life might not fully realize: "Properly speaking, Brooke was not a war poet. His 1914 sonnets do not derive from personal experience of trench warfare on the Western Front" (Wohl, 92). Under this definition a soldier who only wrote poems about Gallipoli would not qualify as a war poet. Even as Wohl ignores Brooke's own experience in Belgium—"by dawn we got into trenches, very good ones, and relieved Belgians" (*L*, 624)— and dismisses its validity, even as he omits Brooke's own realization that his chances of living through the Gallipoli campaign were slim, Wohl elsewhere provides information with which Brooke too was probably familiar: "The younger the junior officer and the more privileged his education, the more likely he was to be killed" (Wohl, 114). Because they were leaders and had to set an example, their rate of death was higher than that of the men they led. Brooke wrote to Cox about the landing at Gallipoli that was called off at the last minute: "Everyone's face looked drawn and ghastly. . . . [M]y company was to be the first to land. . . . I was seized with an agony of remorse that I hadn't taught my platoon a thousand things more energetically and competently" (*L*, 674). The person who died on that French hospital ship was neither a semidivine symbol of youthful poetry nor an ignorant, sloganeering premature Blimp. His reputation was the victim of forces that, while in some sense instigated by him, ultimately were beyond anyone's control.

World War I is singular in several aspects. While literate soldiers had been fighting since the American Civil War, this was the first war in which literate British soldiers largely took part. Previously the vast majority of British armed forces had been culled, one way or another, from the illiterate lower class. William Cobbett taught himself and others to write correctly and forcefully while a soldier in Nova Scotia in the first years of the nineteenth century, but his case was by far the exception. A literate army will produce, at some level, works of literature. The question was, What would these works consist of? Would they be patriotic propaganda, such as Tennyson and Kipling produced? Or would they describe the reality of warfare from a soldier's point of view? The latter, of course, is exactly what happened during World War I, not only because for the first time a large portion of the army was educated and well read but because of the very nature of the war itself. The static nature of the conflict, of men immured for long stretches of time within trenches, with short, savage bursts of combat, gave ample opportunity for both the reading and the writing of literature, especially poetry, as did the long periods of recuperation in a hospital. Other branches of the service did not produce poetry of the quality of Owen's, Sassoon's, or Rosenberg's. There were no great sailor poems (although technically, Brooke was an officer in the navy and commanded a force of former stokers). When World War II began, the question was soon asked, "Where are the war poets?" Although several notable ones eventually would arise, the reason they did not appear as quickly or as frequently as in World War I was the mobile nature of that conflict. The whole concept of warfare initiated by the Wehrmacht in its strategy of blitzkrieg was inimical to the production of the short, almost antilyrical type of poem so often written by the best poets of World War I. The most notable genre of World War II was the novel, particularly those written, like the poetry of World War I, by veterans: Norman Mailer, Joseph Heller, Evelyn Waugh, and James Jones. Poetry was able to succeed so well during World War I because a sizable reading public had been prepared for it, in large part by anthologies such as *Georgian Poetry,* and its success was attributable to the publicizing efforts Brooke had made in behalf of it; one critic has claimed that Brooke was responsible for the fact that the prime minister's limousine was waiting for the first copies of *Georgian Poetry* outside Harold Monro's Poetry Bookstore the day it was published.

As the foregoing discussion shows, this large reading public, both on the home and Western fronts, found Brooke's *1914 and Other Poems* to be extremely satisfying (and not only the war poems; in a letter to his mother Owen quotes offhandedly from "The Great Lover," as if he expected her to be familiar with it as well). Brooke's war poems answered a need in readers for meaning, a justification for the sacrifice they were expected to make—an aspect Dean Inge in his Easter Sermon and Winston Churchill in his obituary of Brooke were quick to fasten on. This need grew even greater as the war progressed, and more and more people grew at first vaguely and then more explicitly doubtful about the war aims of the British government. Macaulay's *Non-Combatants and Others* captures the sense of unease many felt at the war's caesura, so to speak. Why were the British still fighting? Why were so many being lost? Brooke's poems continued to provide an answer; it is sometimes easy to forget that the success of the war's greatest antiwar poet, Wilfred Owen, was not only posthumous but postbellum. One of the unspoken myths about World War I is that those who are now considered to be the greatest poets produced by that conflict were somehow as popular during it as, for instance, Joan Baez was with a certain section of the American population during the Vietnam War. There was significant antiwar sentiment during World War I, mainly centering on the Bloomsbury group and Bernard Shaw, but it was neither sizable nor influential. The soldiers on the Western front had not lost their ideals; indeed, many of them could not, if they wanted to survive psychologi-

cally. Some of these ideals were, in the words of Samuel Hynes describing
R. H. Tawney's, "the idea of fighting a war to save others from war in the
future; of making a lasting, just peace; of defending humanity and democracy" (Hynes 1992, 119). In opposition to this are what Hynes calls
"Rupert Brookeish emotions": "patriotism, enthusiasm, or a desire to die
for one's country" (Hynes 1992, 51). Many would argue, however, that
such emotions are just as necessary as the other, more altruistic war aims
to the fighting and winning of a war. How many works of literature of
World War II foreground or even mention its much more justifiable war
aims of defeating fascism and a nation that mechanized genocide? Even
more than the works of World War I, the works of World War II seem to
proclaim the lesson that Septimus Smith, the veteran of Virginia Woolf's
Mrs. Dalloway, fears to discover: life has no meaning. George Orwell, in his
essays before and during World War II, stressed the need for Hynes's
"Rupert Brookeish" emotions in its participants. The comparison between
Brooke and Orwell will be treated in more detail later, but for now it
needs only be noted that in "My Country Right or Left" Orwell defined
patriotism as a "devotion to something that is changing but is felt to be
mystically the same" (Orwell, 1:539), a theme that could be said to form
the subtext of "The Soldier": "for ever England."

    This transformation of the ideology for what is necessary to fight a
"just" war began during World War I, and Brooke's war poems were
among the first victims of it. Perhaps World War I was only quantifiably
different from previous wars, because of the vast numbers lost on all
sides, but the war was felt by many to be inherently different. Even such
a sympathetic observer as John Lehmann can say of the metaphors in
"Peace," "These are the sentiments of one who had at least had had no
opportunity to face the reality of twentieth-century warfare—killing and
maiming and being killed and maimed in the most appalling ways by
the most devilish devices of terror" (Lehmann, 136). Yet is not all warfare "appalling"? The "devilish devices of terror" are words applied to the
introduction of any new technology in warfare. The "terror" implicit in
World War I was neither being killed by artillery, a possibility that had
existed for centuries, nor being cut down by machine-gun fire, a
prospect that had existed for several decades. The terror lay in the number of names listed in the daily casualty columns of the newspapers and
in the social classes from which for the first time so many of them came.
Thus Brooke's message in the war sonnets came to be seen, in Owen's
phrase from "Dulce et Decorum Est," "the old Lie." The "Lost
Generation" is not entirely a myth. If indeed that generation was not

totally lost—killed—in the war, then those who survived, whether in combat or out of it, felt the guilt implicit in what is psychologically termed survivor's syndrome, and became "lost" in the sense Gertrude Stein meant when she coined the phrase—without direction. As Hynes puts it, "This feeling, that the men who had died were the finest of their generation, and that the fact of their dying somehow proved their wasted excellence, is very common in post-war writing about the war of all kinds. . . . [I]f one had survived, one must have been less than those who died" (Hynes 1992, 317). Such a response initially worked in Brooke's favor, but as the reaction against him set in, it was remembered that he had not "actually" died in combat and so was somehow unworthy of being placed on the honor role. As Wohl puts it, Brooke "had been deprived of the honor of dying in battle by a particularly virulent infection" (Wohl, 92), as if the manner of his death changed its meaning.

Similarly, Brooke's whole attitude toward the war in material other than his poetry has been oversimplified, partly because of his own commitment to, in his words, the "fresh, boyish stunt," in contrast to the grim slaughter that would come later. Brooke's nonchalant pose in some of his letters has been taken as emblematic of the unconscious, fateful ebullience that marked many early English volunteers in World War I. This happens, for instance, in Jonathan Rose's *The Edwardian Temperament*, when he claims that "many onlookers perceived a wonderful outburst of vital energy" at the beginning of the war, and in proof of this quotes: "'I think Life's FAR more romantic than any books,' Rupert Brooke wrote home from the navy, three months before he died."[22] An examination of the entire letter in which this sentence appears (*L*, 653–54), however, shows that the remark, written to Dudley Ward, was actually about the odyssey of a letter Taatamata had sent him from Tahiti (it was given in Tahiti to a man who mailed it from Vancouver, and it then sank in the St. Lawrence River on the *Empress of Ireland* and was underwater for seven months before it was recovered and sent on to Brooke), *not* his experiences training with the Hood battalion. Similarly, Paul Fussell, in his pioneering study *The Great War and Modern Memory*, states: "It is this conception of war as strenuous but entertaining that permeates Rupert Brooke's letters home during the autumn and winter of 1914–15. 'It's all great fun,' he finds" (a phrase Rose also quotes).[23] An examination of the two-paragraph letter to Frances Cornford in which this comment appears (*L*, 625) shows that the body of it, the first paragraph, is a plea to save the Old Vicarage, which Brooke had heard was going to be torn down. The last two-sentence paragraph reads,

"Rain, rain, rain. But it's all great fun." And his complimentary close is "Yours under Mars." The letter is meant to be flip and lighthearted; it is of a piece with the pose he loved to adopt with his oldest and most secure friends. On the same page this comment appears is the tail end of a letter Brooke wrote to Cathleen Nesbitt about the evacuation of Antwerp, in which these sentences appear: "And there we joined the refugees, with all their goods on barrows and carts, in a double line, moving forwards about a hundred yards on hour, white and drawn and beyond emotion. The glare was like hell." The heartiness Brooke adopted, the public school boy bravado, was not a pose confined to Rupert Brooke in the early stages of the war. In Graves's 1916 letter to Marsh about meeting Brooke in a dream, he tells about his injury: "As you may have heard, the old Bosche has punctured me with a 5.9 howitzer shell clean through chest and back, but I'm ridiculously well considering and my cheerfulness and good condition go on improving each other like wild-fire" (Graves, 56). The unspoken ethos in both Brooke's and Graves's case seems to be that any personal discomfort or injury is underplayed and deprecated; however, any injury to others is described sympathetically and dramatically.

The standard portrayal of Rupert Brooke in the early days of World War I is that of an overgrown public school ninny, almost criminal in his blind, unconscious shilling for the Old Men who would send an entire generation off to the slaughterhouses of the Marne and the Somme. In this view, Brooke's blithe "Well, if Armageddon is *on,* I suppose one should be there" is the remark that best sums up his negligent, offhand pretense. Pathetically, his body was too weak to allow him even his dream of dying in battle. Yet the reality is far more complex. Brooke is the chief culprit in the creation of this caricature that has been erected over his literary grave, almost in counterbalance to the overblown statuary over his actual grave on Skyros. Not only did the phrase about Armageddon form the simplistic climax to his much more ambivalent essay about the beginning of the war, "An Unusual Young Man," but he repeated it to such sympathetic listeners as J. C. Squire (Hassall, 459), who would later lead the more epicene brand of Georgian poetry. There were enough such aspects of Brooke that a stick-figure like him did not later have to be invented to set up in contrast to the more complicated sensibilities of the later war poets, the best of whom, out of an almost tragic necessity, did achieve the honorable quietus of dying in battle. The countermyth of Brooke as a sloganeering twit satisfied almost as many needs as did the original myth of Brooke as a slain Apollonian bard. The real Brooke was far more interesting, both in himself and as a representative figure. People need a means of expressing their grief, and it must be consonant with the times. Thus, the simple black granite of the Vietnam memorial and its thousands of names becomes a conduit for grief over the loss of so many in what seemed a futile war; thus, "The Soldier" seemed to express for many, who had already had their religious faith shaken, a mystical reason, a mythical England into which their loved ones had been transformed, in a war for which the original causes were overwhelmed by the magnitude of its suffering. Brooke provided that means, which is the reason for both his praise and his subsequent neglect.

What If . . .

Almost any historic personage who has accomplished anything and died with some of his or her promise unfulfilled has been subjected to what seems to be the most pleasurable yet least verifiable of academic speculations: "What would X have achieved had he or she lived?" In the case of certain figures, such as Rupert Brooke or George Orwell, around whom tendentious and contentious camps have established themselves, the speculations can seem endless. Add to that Brooke's particularly long maturation process, and one has almost a perfect subject on which to project a personal argument or thesis. Too often this has been the case in Brooke studies. Arguments have been proffered with little proof, and when the facts are examined, they are seldom gone into very deeply. Yet the answer to the question of what Brooke would done had he lived will continue to fascinate; as Michael Hastings, far from Brooke's most sympathetic critic, has said, "He had a beginning and that was all; it is the *unfulfillment* in his pleasant, remarkable personality which is of importance and must continue to be" (Hastings, 210, 212).

Perhaps the easiest argument to dispute is one that several friends, most notably Virginia Woolf and D. Pepys Whiteley, have advanced: that Brooke was destined to be a greater writer of prose than poetry. Sometimes these views are vitiated, as Woolf's are, by a concurrent admission that writers like Donne and Dryden were better prose stylists than poets, thus betraying that the inner ear that had judged Brooke's poetry was perhaps not very finely tuned. Brooke was a fine writer of prose when he wanted to be, but too often in *Letters from America* he just seems to run out of gas; he loses interest in a subject and dismisses it. These letters written for the *Westminster Gazette* are not much more meditated on than the letters he wrote about the same places to friends back home. Brooke was essentially a miniaturist, and his probable forte in prose would have been the essay, yet he left surprisingly few examples, outside of reviews and notes for talks. He seems to have felt little desire or ambition to be a prose writer, although he was apparently satisfied by the payment he received from the newspaper for his travel articles. He had no desire to be a man of letters; his comment about the weaknesses of William Morris's theory of universal art—"Better, almost, a literature of blue-books than a literature of belles-lettres" (DA, 6)—reveals his true attitude toward men of letters such as Edmund Gosse. His dismissal of Whitman's and some of Pound's poetry also shows that he personally ranked poetry as the higher, more effective art. Brooke was unsure of how he would make money out of writing poetry (Frances Cornford had to dissuade him from publishing his first volume of poetry out of his own, or rather his mother's, pocket)—indeed, he was unsure at times about his vocation in general. But in the best of all possible worlds, he would have remained a poet who was able "above all, to live poetry."

The most furious arguments naturally arise about what kind of war poetry Brooke would have written had he lived. Many writers about Brooke are sympathetic to his capabilities to grow and adapt, to move beyond rhetoric into the type of more critically acclaimed war verse that Graves, Owen, Sassoon, and Rosenberg wrote. Timothy Rogers, who once planned to write a biography of Brooke, is perhaps the most positive: "The truth is, surely, that no one could have written more bitterly, more ironically, more truly of war than Rupert Brooke. There is small doubt he would have done so, had he lived: he was acutely sensitive to the sorrows and the beastliness of war; his early 'realistic' vein was always near the surface" (Rogers, 10). Unfortunately, the basis for this view is flawed, since Brooke's "realistic" vein was always highly idiosyncratic; it is not the realism of, say, Flaubert or Howells or any other writer usually classified as realistic. Brooke's realism is perhaps better termed "antilyricism," even though that is too weak a term. It is not even a pure "intellectualism," which is what many of the reviewers of Brooke's first volume viewed it as, because of the undercurrent of psychological pressure beneath the surface ("you'll be dirty too!" [PW, 129]); nor is it totally "metaphysical," whatever the affinity Brooke felt for such an inclusive tradition of wit. Perhaps this aspect of Brooke's art could have adapted itself to a more realistic depiction of war than celebrating graves and trumpets, but only if some portion of it engaged the psychological counterbalance that triggered his realism. This is probably what Kenneth Millard means when he writes about Brooke's "more limited experience of war," that "contrary to the suggestion of poems such as 'A Channel Passage' and 'Jealousy' his poetry was ultimately disinclined to take imaginative possession of sordid physical circumstances" (Millard, 57).

Edmund Blunden, himself a war poet, also took a generous view of Brooke's capabilities for adapting to the grimmer circumstances of trench warfare: "That Brooke, if he had lived to march into the horrifying battlefield of the River Ancre with his surviving companions of the Hood Battalion in the deep winter of 1916, would have continued to write sonnets or other poems in the spirit of the "1914" sonnets, is something that I cannot credit."[24] As evidence he cites the "Fragment" that Brooke wrote on his way to the Dardanelles in 1915, which Keynes placed as the frontispiece to Brooke's *Poetical Works*. For Blunden, who edited the poetry of Owen and wrote a memoir of him, the key emotion this fragment reveals is pity, the emotion Owen called the source of his war poetry: "Pity resounds even if ["Fragment"] ends not in pity, not in hero-worship, only in an apprehension of new ghosts, the writer himself soon to be one of them" (Blunden, 21). Even Millard acknowledges the possible connection between Brooke's poetry and Owen's, chiefly in their regard for the body. "Brooke's obsession with inert and grotesque physical circumstances might have acted as a model for Owen's presentation of the body as a collection of anatomical components" (Millard, 170). John Lehmann is another sympathetic observer who believes that Brooke's penchant for poetic realism would have overcome his recent ties to the upper-class establishment: "It seems scarcely possible that this highly sensitive writer, who had shown himself in earlier poems so impatient of decorous pretences, would not have felt challenged, in spite of his new friendships with the politicians and soldiers in high places who were directing the war, to tell the truth about the Gallipoli fighting as Sassoon and Owen were to tell it about the Western Front" (Lehmann, 163). Yet the Gallipoli fighting was of a different order than the drawn-out agony of trench warfare. Brooke's poetry might indeed have changed, but it would not have been the same kind that the more acclaimed war poets began to write. And in 1950 Rose Macaulay, whose attitude toward the war had changed as so many others' had, also declared that "the content of Rupert Brooke's war poetry would have changed utterly. It would have become all that is most disgusted and disillusioned" (Emery, 149).

The number of critics who deny that Brooke's war poetry would have changed in response to further experience is smaller, but their arguments are harder to refute, since their premises are usually based on the entire body of Brooke's work, which is much more sizable than the few realistic poems adduced as evidence by Brooke's defenders. Millard, for instance, claims that despite Brooke's various attempts at broadening the language of his poetic epoch, which Millard sees as Edwardian rather than Georgian, Brooke was incapable of adopting a new diction to adapt to changing circumstance: Brooke is "characteristically Edwardian in his final inability to relinquish the propriety and decorum (the rhetoric) which the Modernists set out to eliminate" (Millard, 179). In his study of the poets of World War I, Michael Crawford sets forth two main reasons for his belief that Brooke would not have developed as a war poet. The first is that Brooke had simply practiced his own aesthetic for too long to grow radically; he would not be able to change his spots: "the highly personalized perspective that he shared with other Georgian poets was part of his make-up long before the war. This would have been likely to endure in a writer who, at twenty-eight, had been conscientiously writing poetry for almost a decade and had already developed his style and his poetic stance." The second reason is that Brooke's experience at Antwerp had done nothing to modify the sentiments that he had already poetically embodied in "1914." Brooke would be able adapt his poetry only if "he could have forsaken both his commitment to Georgian lyricism and his intensely personalized approach to what he observed" (Crawford, 41).

Perhaps the only prediction that can be made about Brooke's further career as a war poet had he survived his illness is that it most likely would have ended on the beaches of Gallipoli. The fragments Keynes included in the *Poetical Works* are maddeningly ambivalent: they can be used to argue both sides of the question. I think the key point to keep in mind is that for the second time in his life (the first being when he replaced his father as headmaster at Rugby), Brooke was in significant charge of a large number of human beings. There was always a segment of his personality that wished to throw off responsibility and wander, but an equally important part of him wanted to assume some sort of leadership, as happened with his involvement in the Marlowe Dramatic Society and the Cambridge University Fabian Society and in his role as informal leader of the neo-pagans at the Old Vicarage. Even as the most junior of officers, Brooke had a responsibility to his men, one he took seriously. He wrote to Cathleen Nesbitt about his fears as he waited to embark on the abortive start of the Gallipoli landings, "I was seized with an agony of remorse that I hadn't taught my platoon a thousand things more energetically and competently" (*L,* 674). The most devastating criticism of the war sonnets is the one made by Sorley the year they were published: that they are ultimately selfish and self-centered, full of what Hynes has called "Brooke's note of endless self-regard" (Hynes 1992, 190). Yet that same quality was the ultimate source of their popularity, as readers applied Brooke's emotions to their own situations, whether as soldiers or as civilians with loved ones at the front. In some of the fragments of his war poetry, Brooke seemed to be ready to move out imaginatively from preoccupation with his own situation to concentrate on the situations of others in war, to emerge from self-pity into true pity, as Blunden says. In the first fragment Keynes selects from the unfinished war poetry, the speaker is contemplating his friends before they go into battle, whom he "would have thought of . . . in pity . . . that / This gay machine of splendour'ld soon be broken" but for the fact that they are actually "coloured shadows . . . Slight bubbles" (*PW*, 17). In the "Nobby Clark" fragment at the end of the Poetical Works, he contemplates the death of a stoker in battle, who tried to "stop a shrapnel with his belly" and "went out . . . Upon the illimitable dark" (*PW*, 205). Brooke's problem is that he is still fixated on what happens after death; his search for a substitute for the Christian heaven in "The Soldier" is precisely what Dean Inge took him to task for in his Easter sermon. If Brooke could have moved beyond that, to concentrate on the fact of death in battle, "the weight and firmness And link'd beauty of bodies . . . Thought little of, pashed, scattered . . ." (*PW*, 17), then he could have developed as a war poet. It must always be kept in mind, however, that had Brooke survived not only his illness but the carnage of the beaches of Gallipoli, he probably would have assumed a position on General Hamilton's staff, and any such development would have been arrested and all his worst tendencies easily have reemerged.

In fact, some of the more unusual speculations about Brooke's possible future have posited that he might not have been continued as a poet at all. Remembering his interest in politics and his immense personal charm, some of his friends thought his future lay in politics. Virginia Woolf wrote to Gwen Raverat that she felt his possibilities were limitless: "He was, I thought, the ablest of all the young men; I did not then think much of his poetry, which he read aloud on the lawn, but I thought he would be Prime Minister, because he had such a gift with people, and such sanity, and such force." Of course, Woolf's conjectures were heavily influenced by her negative judgment of Brooke's poetry, and her referring to Brooke's "sanity" reveals that she is perhaps tailoring her opinions to those of her correspondent, as she did with Brooke's mother: "My idea was that he was to be a Member of Parliament and edit the Classics, a very powerful, ambitious man, but not a poet" (Woolf, 1977a, 3:178). Brooke, however, did not seem much interested in the classics after Cambridge, other than to parade his knowledge in front of his less well-educated friends, particularly women. Philip Larkin suggested a future career for Brooke along similar lines. Larkin's view of Brooke after reading his *Letters* was that Brooke "was a vigorous, practical and self-interested character whose short life was a continual approximation towards knowing this. If he had not moved in the heady atmosphere of Edwardian Cambridge, he would have realized it sooner." In other words, Larkin accepts Brooke's own post-Lulworth self-evaluation. Although Larkin was generous in his selection of Brooke's poems in his edition of *The Oxford Book of Twentieth Century English Poetry*,[25] he too feels that had Brooke survived, "there seems small likelihood that he would have found sufficient fulfillment in writing verse." Like Woolf, he posits a political future for Brooke, but he, perhaps waggishly, offers another possible venue for success: "With his political ideas and good looks, he might have become leader of the Liberal Party, or even (being his mother's son) succeeded Arnold in the headmastership of Rugby" (Larkin, 181). Perhaps had Brooke been able to sustain an internal equanimity, he would have ventured off into other careers. But as long as he felt that periodic internal compulsion to "above all, to *live* poetry," he probably would have continued to write it.

Brooke's Place

Where exactly does Rupert Brooke fit in the history of twentieth-century poetry? Was he an inescapably minor figure, who had already done his best work, as weak as that was? As Ronald Pearsall puts it, "his slight talent had not only peaked, but moved along in its downward curve" (Pearsall, 150). Or had the trends of his time already passed him by? In the words of Gloria Fromm, about Delaney's book, which appeared at the centenary of Brooke's birth, "not even his salvaging operation, performed with such skill, could hope to succeed: the patient is not simply dead but obsolete" (Fromm, 77). Yet if Brooke is to be thought of as a minor figure, then very few minor figures have had so many polemics fought over the siting of their literary gravesites, not to mention all the seemingly extraliterary wranglings over the politics of the war sonnets and the revelations about Brooke's private life. While these controversies are to some extraliterary, every argument over the war sonnets or the propriety or relevance of Brooke's psychological condition only serves to affirm the power of art in the first case, and to continue the dialogue over the relationship between life and art in the second. At any rate, no ineluctably minor figure would have so many speculations over what he would have done had he lived. Every discussion of Brooke's possibilities is based on the capabilities he showed during life, a capacity for change that some saw as a sign of weakness (Brooke as "chameleon") and others as a potentiality for growth and maturity. There is little doubt that Brooke during the last year of his life did show signs of finally growing up; however, he never did reach the stage that James Barrie talked about in the last words of Peter Pan, the stage directions as Wendy leaves him and flies away home. "If he could get the hang of the thing his cry might become 'To live would be an awfully big adventure!' but he can never quite get the hang of it, and so no one is as gay as he" (Barrie, 94). Brooke never got to the point where he could accept life on its own terms.

The controversies over "1914," as well as the caricature of Georgian poetry that was established early on in the modernist period, as the weaknesses and affectations of later Georgianism were grafted onto earlier Georgian works, have obscured Brooke's true importance as a transitional figure. Some of his friends recognized this immediately after his death. Lascelles Abercrombie, in an obituary in the *Morning Post*, wrote, "many hoped he was destined to reconcile in himself the old traditional style of lyric poetry in England . . . and that which is so much for the needs of the future that some call it Futurism" (Hastings, 185). In other words, Brooke was a bridge between traditional lyric poetry of the time—Georgianism—and what was soon to be called modernism. Even a critic like Millard recognizes Brooke's attempt, although he denies Brooke any success; Brooke "recognized the transitional nature of his time and made concerted efforts to liberate the thematic range of poetry. . . . It was for the Modernists however to open up the ground at which he had tentatively scratched, and the death of Brooke's generation heralds their advent" (Millard, 180). What exactly, however, was Brooke's generation? Born in 1887, he was five years younger than Virginia Woolf and James Joyce, two years younger than Ezra Pound and D. H. Lawrence, and one year older than T. S. Eliot. Brooke was, if anything, almost an exact literary coeval of the "generation" of modernism, if it can be said to have one, and while this does not make him a modernist, it reminds us that the influences of the times, its zeitgeist, operated as much on him as on any of the other more radical artistic figures.

The most fruitful comparison that can be between Brooke and a modernist is to T. S. Eliot, as Brooke's one-time opponent, Ezra Pound, hinted at. Brooke "was the best of the younger English, though Eliot is certainly more interesting" (Stock, 242). William York Tindall also noticed the similarities between Brooke and Eliot: "Brooke was the most talented of the Georgians, and had he lived he might have developed along the lines of T. S. Eliot, finding in the wit of Donne a vehicle suited to our divided times."[26] Anyone who studies Brooke's later literary interests is immediately struck by their similarities to Eliot's, particularly their affinity for the poetry of Donne and the dramas of Webster. (Brooke and Eliot knew each other slightly; Brooke had introduced Eliot to Harold Monro.) Sometimes the congruences seem uncanny. In a letter to Frances Cornford, Brooke quotes from *The Tempest,* "This music crept by me upon the waters" (*L,* 197), a line Eliot also uses in *The Waste Land* (Eliot 1971, 45). Similarly, in his dissertation on Webster Brooke concentrates on the line "Is the wind in that door still" from *The Devil's Law-Case* and says it has "something of the terror and ghostliness" of other scenes in Elizabethan tragedies (*JW,* 109), effects to which Eliot puts the same line in *The Waste Land* (Eliot 1971, 40). A page later Brooke comments that a character's flinging herself madly to the ground and lying there is a convention of revenge plays and "goes back . . . to old Hieronomo himself" (*JW,* 110); Hieronomo, of course, also appears in the last lines of *The Waste Land* (Eliot 1971, 50). And in "An Unusual Young Man," the young man remembers among his experiences in Germany "the swish of evening air in the face, as one skis down past the pines . . . the quiet length of evening over the Starnberger-See" (*LFA,* 174), incidents echoed also in the first section of *The Waste Land* (Eliot 1971, 37). One critic, in fact, finds correspondences between the desiccated opening lines of *The Waste Land* and the lush English countryside in Brooke's "Grantchester": "When the openings to *The Waste Land* and 'Grantchester' are compared it can be seen that there are considerable likenesses in detail and design; and it is likely that Eliot would be expecting the reader to catch the essential dissimilarity between their two views of life, as glimpsed through their accounts of Spring memories and awakenings."[27] That Eliot intended this specific allusion, however, seems a tenuous inference at best, unless in the broader sense that the barren scene at the beginning of *The Waste Land* is meant to stand in opposition to the fecundity celebrated in all Georgian poetry, not merely the "unofficial rose" of "Grantchester." The correspondences between Brooke and Eliot that I've cited here are not meant to be read as allu-

sions, references, or even influences; they rather seem to be the result of
two poetic sensibilities on curiously parallel tracks, as with the father's
querulous complaints in *Lithuania,* "What are you both thinking? I
Don't know what you're thinking" (*Li,* 365), and the subdued hysteria
of the questions of the female speaker in the second section of *The Waste
Land* (Eliot 1971, 40). Each poet, however, produced much different
results.

The similarities extend to their biographies. Both poets were dominat-
ed by mothers; Eliot seemed to be so more willingly. Peter Ackroyd
describes Eliot's mother as "a Fabian of American life."[28] Both were
impressed at an early age by James Thomson's long poem "City of
Dreadful Night"; they were also interested in the poetry of the aesthetes,
Brooke to a much more damaging extent. Both poets in their early poetry evinced a distrust of women; Ackroyd says that in Eliot's "first schoolboy poetry the theme had been of love withered and decayed" (Ackroyd,
327), and about Eliot's early unpublished poetry of around 1911, "the
images of women are of those who destroy his self-possession and elicit
from him feeling of self-disgust" (Ackroyd, 44), all of which can be
applied to Brooke's verse. Although Eliot enjoyed the summer he spent in
Germany in 1914, he felt an exile there; the original title of
"Grantchester," written in Germany, was "The Sentimental Exile." Both
poets were neurasthenic to a significant degree: Brooke used his various
attacks of conjunctivitis to relieve himself of stress; Eliot complained of
exhaustion for most of his life. Both had nervous breakdowns and were
treated by famous neurological experts; Brooke in Cannes after Lulworth,
Eliot at Lausanne. Both were artistically ambitious, and both had literary
"patrons": Eliot, Pound; Brooke, Marsh. Eliot's friends complained that
he compartmentalized his life; so did Brooke's. Both were anti-Semitic,
and in both cases friends or biographers have linked this tendency to their
feelings about women. Ackroyd says about Eliot during the 1920s, "it
was a period when his own personality threatened to break apart, and it
seems likely that his distrust of Jews and women was the sign of an
uneasy and vulnerable temperament in which aggression and insecurity
were compounded" (Ackroyd, 304). Many of Brooke's friends thought his
anti-Semitism was exacerbated by the Lulworth crisis, which also intensified his antipathy toward women. In his more mature relationships with
women, Eliot was "disturbed and disgusted by female sexuality," and he
"established relationships with women in which the dominant note was
one of camaraderie not unmixed with his desire for comfort or protection"
(Ackroyd, 310); Brooke's attitudes toward women were much the same

mixture of puritanism and a desire for maternal safekeeping. Both poets were accused of playing roles, of assuming the guise of various characters in their relationships with others.

The more striking similarities occur in their treatment of subjects, authors, and periods they shared an interest in. Eliot himself praised Brooke's "The Fish." They both reviewed Herbert Grierson's edition of Donne's poetry within a week of each other. As Timothy Rogers has pointed out, their analyses unconsciously echoed each other's. Eliot said, "Soul and body are what Donne has to offer with their subtle and secret interactions" (Rogers 1971, 16); Brooke claimed that Donne "was the one English love-poet who was not afraid to acknowledge that he was composed of body, soul, and mind" (*PRB,* 92). As Joseph Duncan remarks, "Some of Brooke's critical essays strikingly suggest those of Eliot in their sensitive insight, style, and treatment of similar ideas." In Brooke's reviews of Grierson's edition of Donne, "he gave a preliminary formulation to ideas which Eliot was to treat more definitively in the 1920's."[29] Further, in his dissertation on Webster Brooke analyzes Webster's method of using scraps and snippets of the ideas and images of other authors in writing his own plays (a method very much like Eliot's in composing *The Waste Land*): "The advantage of this method is that you unconsciously transmute all 'borrowed' ideas to harmony with your own personality—that when you hunt them out to reclaim them you find them slightly changed" (*JW,* 154). This is very similar to Eliot's use in "Tradition and the Individual Talent" of the famous simile of the catalyst, in which two gases are transmuted into sulfurous acid, to show how the weight of tradition influences the poet's creativity: "The poet's mind is in fact a receptacle for seizing and storing up numberless feelings, phrases, and images, which remain there until all the particles which can unite to form a new compound are present together."[30] In the same way, Brooke proposed a fissure that took place in English literature similar to Eliot's famous "dissociation of sensibility," although Brooke gives it a much earlier date. "The true gap is far more remarkable and far earlier. It is hidden by over-lappings, but its presence is obvious about the year 1611. . . . Heart supplanted brain, and senses sense" (*JW,* 72). Not only had tragedy flourished in the years immediately preceding that date, but "the intellect and the imagination had been dizzily and joyfully up-borne on that wit," and Brooke proceeds to give his favorite definition of metaphysical wit, Chapman's—it "can make anything of anything" (*JW,* 72). In his essay on Philip Massinger, Eliot makes a similar judgment: "And indeed, with the end of Chapman, Middleton, Webster, Tourneur,

Donne we end a period when the intellect was immediately at the tips of the senses" (Eliot 1975, 156). For Eliot, in "The Metaphysical Poets," Donne and Herbert are "intellectual poets" whose minds were "constantly amalgamating disparate experience. . . . [I]n the mind of the poet these experiences are always forming new wholes." The poets of the early 1600s "possessed a mechanism of sensibility which could devour any kind of experience" (Eliot 1975, 64). Of course, this literary "age of gold" was one to which both Brooke and Eliot were attempting to return in their own works, by expanding the range of "acceptable" poetic subject matter, images, and language. For a variety of reasons, not the least of which were that he did not fight in the war and lived through it, Eliot was far more successful.

Eliot's and Brooke's interest in Webster is illustrative of not only their poetic agendas but also their personalities. Eliot's most famous reference to Webster is the passage in "Whispers of Immortality" about the dramatist's ability "to see the skull beneath the skin" because he "was much possessed by death" (Eliot 1971, 32). In Brooke's words Webster "was, more particularly, obsessed by the idea of the violence of the moment of death" (*JW*, 156). They both noted and admired the fact that Webster allowed himself a wide latitude in constructing his blank verse; Eliot says that "Webster is much freer than Shakespeare" (Eliot 1975, 34), and Brooke that Webster was "probably the freest" (*JW*, 124). The interior psychological motivations for Brooke's and Eliot's affinity for Webster seems to be that they were both fascinated by the intensity of his scenes. Other Elizabethan and Jacobean playwrights had written tragedies with plots just as grim; it is Webster's power in the climactic scenes of his plays that attracts them. Brooke notes that "Webster, more than any man in the world, has caught the soul in the second of its decomposition in death, when knowledge seems transcended, and the darkness closes in, and boundaries fall away" (*JW*, 101); Eliot, that Webster's "breastless creatures under ground / Leaned backward with a lipless grin" (Eliot 1971, 32).

The ultimate question, of course remains: if these two poets were so similar, then why is their verse so different, both in focus and in quality? For one, even though they both enjoyed Thomson's lurid depiction of a ruined metropolis, Brooke could not bring himself to use an urban setting for any of his better poems, no matter how much he praised urban life to Germans he met. Eliot was extremely successful in portraying the desiccation and alienation of twentieth-century urban dwellers in "The Love Song of J. Alfred Prufrock" and *The Waste Land*. For another,

Brooke was much more of a traditionalist than Eliot. His experimenta-
tion was limited to the subject matter of his "unpleasant" poems. His
prejudice in favor of rhythm and form put him outside the mainstream
of modernism. Most important, however, are the ways in which both
poets handled and used their internal psychological stress, which in both
cases seems to have been related to a similar attitude toward women.
Eliot had much greater control over his feelings—so great, in fact, that
his problem was diagnosed as aboulie, a paralysis of will, and his therapy
by Dr. Roger Vittoz at Lausanne sometimes involved merely attempting
to lift his arm from a chair. When Eliot learned to free himself from his
own "mind-forg'd" restraints, he wrote, with great ease and fluidity, the
last section of *The Waste Land*. Brooke's problem was similar. There were
a great many acts which to him were a violation of his inner puritanism,
and he punished himself for every self-aware loss of restraint, such as his
affair with Ka Cox. Because his punishment always came after the act,
he did not learn how to live with his inner web of constraints. Millard
claims that "it is possible to argue that Brooke's contradictions and
incongruities went unresolved not merely because he died young, but
because he had a genuine and profound affinity with the Renaissance
mind" (Millard, 172). It was, however, not his mind but his personality
that was contradictory. The union of body, spirit, and intellect that
Brooke found so attractive in Donne, that was a hallmark of what to
Brooke was a literary Edenic period, was also Brooke's psychological
goal. Eliot was able to distance himself enough from his own psychological difficulties to use the phrases, images, and language from his reading
as a catalyst with which to produce his own works. In the famous declaration near the end of "Tradition and the Individual Talent," he defines
this process: "Poetry is not a turning loose of emotion, but an escape
from emotion; it is not the expression of personality, but an escape from
personality. But, of course, only those who have personality and emotions know what it means to want to escape from these things" (Eliot
1975, 43). Brooke never learned this; his poems, for instance, on his voy-
age to the South Seas show him prodding the injured areas of his psyche
to see if they still hurt. "Grantchester" is like *The Waste Land* in that both
are amalgams of sections of disparate tones and attitudes, but while
Pound's skillful editing helped make this aspect of *The Waste Land* seem
artful and controlled, Brooke's lack of control of tone in "Grantchester"
denies that poem any sense of distance from its speaker, the sense of
irony that is so highly prized in Eliot's works. Brooke seemed to want to

escape from his own personality, but he never learned to do it in his art; Eliot did so, triumphantly.

Thus, while Brooke is much more of a transitional figure than he has formerly been given credit for, the question of whether he would have been able to become a "bridge" between the modernist and Georgian branches of twentieth-century English poetry is problematic. The answer depends on Brooke's capacity for change, a capacity that many of his critics would deny him because of his "regression" at the beginning of World War I, his apparent assumption of the Victorian values he had fought against for so long. Yet in analyzing Brooke's patriotism at the beginning of World War I, it is important to compare his case with that of another socialist at the start of England's next world war—George Orwell. Like Brooke, Orwell thought himself surrounded by a class of intellectuals possessed of little if any patriotism or common sense. They had switched allegiances and loyalties whenever Stalin changed the party line from Moscow: "It is all very well to be 'advanced' and 'enlightened,' to snigger at Colonel Blimp and proclaim your emancipation from all traditional loyalties, but a time comes when the sand of the desert is sodden red and what have I done for thee, England, my England? As I was brought up in this tradition myself I can recognise it under strange disguises, and also sympathize with it, for even at its stupidest and most sentimental it is a comelier thing than the shallow self-righteousness of the left-wing intelligentsia" (Orwell, 1:535). Brooke himself several times declared, with only a slight snigger, that he agreed with the Henley poem to which Orwell alludes—for instance, in 1909: "Yet England ('my England' [Henley]), is, to use an old-fashioned word, nice" (*L,* 165). Brooke was also heavily influenced by Hilaire Belloc's view of England. He wrote to Jacques Raverat in 1908: "'England! my England!' in the superb words of the late W. E. Henley. . . . As Mr. Belloc says 'She (England, I mean) is to remain.' I am persuaded she is to remain" (*L,* 122). Unlike the members of Bloomsbury or most Fabians, Brooke increasingly came to believe in an old-fashioned patriotism, which was nevertheless not in the least jingoistic. Brooke never seems to have given up his socialist convictions. He was deeply interested in a workers' strike in Dublin in 1914. Some critics cannot picture any kind of a socialist holding such retrograde, primitive beliefs as patriotism; John Lehmann, for instance, asserts, "It does not appear that . . . his final patriotic convictions had anything to do with his one-time Fabian ardour" (Lehmann, 119). Yet in December of 1914 Brooke wrote to

Reginald Pole, "I'm all in favor of shooting the rich & tyrannical here, beginning with Sir Edgar Speyer" (*L,* 639). Brooke's Fabianism became muted when he began to consort with the circle around Edward Marsh, but that is not to say he abandoned it completely.

Since Brooke's time, it has become a commonplace to take for granted that anyone who is "intellectual" also leans toward pacifism. Orwell alluded to this when he declared that "almost any English intellectual would feel more ashamed of standing to attention during 'God Save the King' than of stealing from a poor box" (Orwell, 2:75). The reason for this, according to Orwell, is the intellectual's fundamental view of the basis for human conduct: "Nearly all western thought since the last war, certainly all 'progressive' thought, has assumed tacitly that human beings desire nothing beyond ease, security, and the avoidance of pain" (Orwell, 2:14). Thus, patriotism, love of country, the concept of self-sacrifice—"Rupert Brookeish emotions"—are all discarded as rational causes for human behavior. Still, Orwell, writing in the midst of World War II, argued that "Men die in battle—not gladly, of course, but at any rate voluntarily—because of abstractions called 'honour,' 'duty,' 'patriotism,' and so forth" (Orwell, 2:17). These are the very abstractions Brooke extols in "1914," for which he has been hooted down ever since. As Hynes notes, "One reason for the popularity of Rupert Brooke's war sonnets is that he got all the abstractions into seventy lines of verse: Holiness, Love, Pain, Honour, Nobleness, Glory, Heroism, Sacrifice, England—they're all there" (Hynes 1992, 109). Most critics after World War I did not admit that these emotions are necessary or even desirable. As Orwell said, people who do believe in such abstractions "are aware of some organism greater than themselves, stretching into the future and the past, within which they feel themselves to be immortal" (Orwell, 2:17)—in Brooke's phrase, "That is for ever England." Orwell quotes a similar patriotic tag: "'Who dies if England lives' sounds like a piece of bombast, but if you alter 'England' to whatever you prefer, you can see that it expresses one of the main motives of human conduct" (Orwell, 2:17). This is the emotion Brooke was referring to when he wrote to Raverat in December 1914, about the same time he was composing the war sonnets, "But there's a ghastly sort of apathy over half the country. And I really think large numbers of male people don't want to die; which is odd" (*L,* 637). The problem for Brooke's reputation has always been that the general view of Brooke has held that such a statement must mean Brooke was wondering why the rest of the men in England didn't want to share in his death wish, not that he was bemoaning their lack of patriotism.

Orwell has not been as excoriated as Brooke was for expressing similar sentiments, because, of course, history has shown that the World War II was a more "justifiable" war than World War I. Also, the intellectuals that Orwell criticized for their abrupt about-face when Hitler and Stalin signed the Nonaggression Pact in 1939 have not been held in as high esteem as the intellectuals Brooke criticized for lacking patriotic zeal in 1914. Kingsley Martin, say, is no Lytton Strachey. For example, Robert Wohl says that "many of the country's keenest minds had begun to call into question" (Wohl, 92) World War I at the time of Brooke's death, and Hynes writes about Brooke's chief targets, "Bloomsbury then, from the war's very beginning, was a continuing demonstration of the fact that opposition to the war—continuous, principled opposition—was a possible attitude for intelligent English men and women" (Hynes 1992, 84). And because Brooke's reaction against Bloomsbury was so violent ("and Rupert wrote [James Strachey] a furious and totally unbalanced letter, saying that he was a bugger and as a bugger he couldn't distinguish between good and bad or understand the actions and responsibilities of normal people: he had not grown up" [Lehmann, 17]), his more rational criticism of its position has been overlooked. In a letter to Ka Cox written en route to the Dardanelles, Brooke discussed a *Working Men's College Journal* which a friend of his had given him, with a lecture in it by E. M. Forster, evidently about the war. Brooke concedes that Forster is "far nicer than most of them" but still, it seems, uninvolved: "The point of war is that it *brings out* their *exteriority*. . . . They're like nice and nasty children outside a circus, who alternately try to peep under the flaps and explain to each other how they despise circuses." Forster is "nice about the soul of man, But oh! doesn't he *suspect* that the nobilities he whinnies for, come out more in war than in peace?" (*L,* 674). Orwell too noted "the spiritual need for patriotism and the military virtues, for which, however little the boiled rabbits of the Left may like them, no substitute has as yet been found" (Orwell, 1:540), and also claimed, "The Bloomsbury highbrow, with his mechanical snigger, is as out-of-date as the cavalry colonel" (Orwell, 2:75).

In "An Unusual Young Man" Brooke attempted to paint a picture of the England he loved and came to value more highly as it was threatened by war: "Grey, uneven little fields, and small, ancient hedges rushed before him, wild flowers, elms and beeches, gentleness, sedate

houses of red brick, proudly unassuming, a countryside of rambling hills
and friendly copses" (*LFA,* 178), a description that Orwell's old class-
mate Cyril Connolly ridiculed as being a return to the womb. Yet it is
very similar to the paean Orwell addressed to the English countryside
when, like Brooke, he returned to it from abroad at the end of *Homage to
Catalonia:* "Down here it was the England I had known in my childhood:
the railway-cuttings smothered in wild-flowers, the deep meadows
where the great shining horses browse and meditate, the slow-moving
streams bordered by willows, the green bosoms of the elms, the lark-
spurs in the cottage gardens." Both of these visions of England are of a
mystical place that will seemingly last forever, that paradoxically has to
be shattered by the outbreak of war to continue to exist. Orwell calls it
"the deep, deep sleep of England, from which I sometimes fear that we
shall never wake till we are jerked out of it by the roar of bombs."[31]
Brooke writes, "I've been praying for a German raid" (*L,* 637). The idea
of war as purgative or cleansing may indeed be pernicious, but it was not
confined merely to the first months of World War I. The idea of patriotism may be outmoded and narcissistic, but it was not only sung about
in "1914." Orwell points out that the young English radical poets of the
Spanish civil war were, in their patriotic emotions, "public school to the
core" (Orwell, 1:540), and the one poet he does name is John
Cornford—the son of Brooke's old friends Francis and Frances Cornford.
John Cornford's full given name—and irony seems too pallid a word to
apply this fact—was Rupert John Cornford.

The real Rupert Brooke was not the golden-haired Apollo; nor was he
the overgrown public school boy patriot; nor was he the psychologically
tormented paranoiac of Lulworth. The real Rupert Brooke deserves to be
viewed in the context of his times and in the totality of his personality
and achievements; that this has not happened is partly the fault of himself and his friends and the protectors of his reputation, partly the result
of the war he happened to defend. If the various false avatars of Brooke
did not exist, then someone would have had to invent them, as much as
he continually reinvented himself. That he seemed to be approaching the
most authentic version of himself just as he died is perhaps the real
tragedy of his death and life.

Notes

Preface

1. Christopher Hassall, *Rupert Brooke: A Biography* (New York: Harcourt, Brace & World, 1964), 187; hereafter cited in text.

2. In a talk at Oxford during World War II, Dylan Thomas satirically referred to the resemblance between the language of some of the politically committed "Auden Generation" and Georgian rhetoric when he said, "I'd like to have talked about a book of poems I've been given to review, a young poet called Rupert Brooke—it's surprising how he has been influenced by Stephen Spender"; in Andrew Motion, *Philip Larkin: A Writer's Life* (New York: Farrar Straus Giroux, 1993), 71.

Chapter One

1. George Orwell, "Why I Write," in *The Collected Essays, Journalism and Letters of George Orwell* (New York: Harcourt Brace Jovancovich, 1968), 1:6; hereafter cited in text.

2. Paul Delaney, *The Neo-Pagans* (New York: Fress Press, 1987), 9; hereafter cited in text.

3. Gloria Fromm, "Saving Rupert Brooke," *New Criterion* 6 (September 1987): 76; hereafter cited in text.

4. Paul Levy, *Moore: G. E. Moore and the Cambridge Apostles* (1979; London: Papermac, 1989), 262; hereafter cited in text.

5. Rupert Brooke, *The Letters of Rupert Brooke,* ed. G. Keynes (New York: Harcourt, Brace & World, 1968), 56; hereafter cited in text as *L.*

6. Norman and Jeanne MacKenzie, *The Fabians* (New York: Simon & Schuster, 1977), 372.

7. Rupert Brooke and Noel Olivier, *Song of Love: The Letters of Rupert Brooke and Noel Olivier,* ed. Pippa Harris (New York: Crown, 1991), 22; hereafter cited in text as *SOL.*

8. The letter is given in Delaney, 78–80.

9. Leonard Woolf, *Beginning Again* (New York: Harcourt Brace Jovanovich, 1972), 18; hereafter cited in text as L. Woolf.

10. Rupert Brooke. *The Prose of Rupert Brooke,* ed. Christopher Hassall (London: Sidgwick & Jackson, 1956), 162; hereafter cited in text as *PRB.*

11. Virginia Woolf, *The Letters of Virginia Woolf,* ed. Nigel Nicolson and Joanne Trautmann (New York: Harcourt Brace Jovanovich, 1977), 3:415; hereafter cited in text as V. Woolf 1977a.

12. Michael Holroyd, *Lytton Strachey: A Biography* (New York: Holt, Rinehart & Winston, 1968), 1:449.
13. Virginia Woolf, *The Diary of Virginia Woolf,* ed. Anne Olivier Bell (New York: Harcourt Brace Jovanovich, 1978), 2:229.
14. J. M. Barrie, *The Plays of J. M. Barrie* (New York: Scribner's, 1950), 30; hereafter cited in text.
15. Rupert Brooke, *Letters from America* (New York: Scribner's, 1916), 69; hereafter cited in text as *LFA.*
16. Cathleen Nesbitt, *A Little Love and Good Company* (Owings Mills, Md.: Stemmer House, 1977), 75.
17. Arthur Stringer, *Red Wine of Youth* (Indianapolis: Bobbs-Merrill, 1948), 205.
18. Robert Brainard Pearsall, *Rupert Brooke: The Man and Poet* (Amsterdam: Rodopi, 1974), 40; hereafter cited in text.
19. Timothy Rogers, *Rupert Brooke: A Reappraisal and Selection from His Writings, Some Hitherto Unpublished* (New York: Barnes & Noble, 1971), 36; hereafter cited in text.
20. Samuel Hynes, "Rupert Brooke," *Edwardian Occasions* (Oxford: Oxford University Press, 1972), 145, hereafter cited in text as Hynes 1972.
21. Jon Stallworthy, *Wilfred Owen* (London: Oxford University Press, 1974), 140n; hereafter cited in text.

Chapter Two

1. Rupert Brooke, *The Poetical Works of Rupert Brooke,* ed. Geoffrey Keynes (London: Faber & Faber, 1946, 1970); hereafter cited in text as *PW.*
2. James Joyce, *A Portrait of the Artist as a Young Man* (Harmondsworth: Penguin, 1977), 247.
3. Robert H. Ross, *The Georgian Revolt: 1910–1922* (Carbondale: Southern Illinois University Press, 1965), 98; hereafter cited in text.
4. Samuel Hynes, *A War Imagined: The First World War and English Culture* (New York: Collier, 1992); hereafter cited in text as Hynes 1992.
5. Myron Simon, *The Georgian Poetic* (Berkeley: University of California Press, 1975), 48.
6. Kenneth Millard, "Rupert Brooke: 'The strife of limbs,'" in *Edwardian Poetry* (Oxford: Clarendon Press, 1991), 168–69; hereafter cited in text.
7. John Drinkwater, "Rupert Brooke," in *The Muse in Council* (Boston: Houghton Mifflin, 1925), 280; hereafter cited in text.
8. Alan Walker Read, "Onomastic Devices in the Poetry of Rupert Brooke," *Literary Onomastic Studies* 9 (1982): 196.
9. Edgar Allen Poe, "The Poetic Principle," in *Essays and Reviews* (1850; New York: Library of America, 1984), 71.

10. Bernard Bergonzi, *Heroes' Twilight: A Study of the Literature of the Great War* (New York: Coward McCann, 1965), 39; hereafter cited in text.

11. Michael Hastings, *The Handsomest Young Man in England: Rupert Brooke* (London: Michael Joseph, 1967), 150; hereafter cited in text.

12. W. H. Auden, *The English Auden,* ed. Edward Mendelson (New York: Random House, 1977), 207.

13. John Donne, *The Complete Poetry of John Donne,* ed. John Shawcross (Garden City, N.Y.: Anchor Books, 1967), 344.

14. Hilaire Belloc, *The Four Men: A Farrago* (1911; Oxford: Oxford University Press, 1984), 161.

15. Wilfred Owen, *The Collected Poems of Wilfred Owen,* ed. C. Day Lewis (New York: New Directions, 1965), 31; hereafter cited in text.

Chapter Three

1. Virginia Woolf, "The Intellectual Imagination," in *The Essays of Virginia Woolf,* ed. Andrew McNellie (New York: Harcourt Brace Jovanovich, 1988), 3:135.

2. Virginia Woolf, *The Letters of Virginia Woolf,* ed. Nigel Nicolson and Joanne Trautmann (New York: Harcourt Brace Jovanovich, 1980), 6:31–32.

3. Timothy Rogers, "Rupert Brooke: Man and Monument," *English* 17 (Autumn 1968): 82–83.

4. Philip Larkin, "The Apollo Bit," in *Required Writing: Miscellaneous Pieces 1955–1982* (New York: Farrar Straus Giroux, 1984), 178; hereafter cited in text.

5. John Lehmann, *The Strange Destiny of Rupert Brooke* (New York: Holt, Rinehart & Winston 1981), 74; hereafter cited in text.

6. Rupert Brooke, *John Webster and the Elizabethan Drama* (New York: Russell & Russell, 1916), 2; hereafter cited in text as *JW.*

7. C. K. Ogden and I. A. Richards, *The Meaning of Meaning* (New York: Harcourt, Brace, 1947), 141.

8. Joseph Conrad, *Heart of Darkness* (New York: Norton, 1971), 5.

9. Virginia Woolf, "Modern Fiction," *The Common Reader* (New York: Harcourt, Brace & World, 1950), 154.

10. T. S. Eliot, "Whispers of Immortality," in *The Complete Poems and Plays: 1909–1950* (New York: Harcourt, Brace & World, 1971), 32; hereafter cited in text as Eliot 1971.

11. Rupert Brooke, *Lithuania,* in *Thirty Famous One Act Plays,* ed. Bennett Cerf and Van Cartmell (Garden City, N.Y.: Garden City), 361; hereafter cited in text as *Li.*

12. Peter Conrad, *Imagining America* (New York: Oxford University Press, 1980); hereafter cited in text.

13. Rupert Brooke, *Democracy and the Arts* (London: Rupert Hart-Davis, 1946), 1; hereafter cited in text as *DA.*

14. See the discussion in Mackenzie about the conflict between the Fabians who believed in an alliance with the trade unions and those who believed in legislation.

15. Cyril Connolly, *Enemies of Promise* (New York: Persea Books, 1983), 15.

Chapter Four

1. Robert Graves and Laura Riding, *A Survey of Modernist Poetry* (1928; New York: Haskell House, 1968), 120.

2. Walter de la Mare, *Rupert Brooke and the Intellectual Imagination* (London: Sidgwick & Jackson, 1919), 31.

3. Ezra Pound, "Our Contemporaries," *Blast* 2 (July 1915): 21.

4. Ezra Pound, *The Selected Letters of Ezra Pound 1907–1941,* ed. D. D. Paige, (1950; New York: New Directions, 1971), 59; hereafter cited in text.

5. Ezra Pound, letter to Milton Bronner, quoted in Noel Stock, *The Life of Ezra Pound* (New York: Avon, 1974), 242; hereafter cited in text as Stock.

6. Virginia Woolf, *The Diary of Virginia Woolf,* ed. Anne Olivier Bell (New York: Harcourt Brace Jovanovich, 1977), 1:171; hereafter cited in text as V. Woolf 1977b.

7. Virginia Woolf, *The Letters of Virginia Woolf,* ed. Nigel Nicolson and Joanee Trautmann (New York: Harcourt Brace Jovanovich, 1976), 2:271.

8. Virginia Woolf, *The Diary of Virginia Woolf,* ed. Anne Olivier Bell (New York: Harcourt Brace Jovanovich, 1978), 2:274.

9. Virginia Woolf, *The Diary of Virginia Woolf,* ed. Anne Olivier Bell (New York: Harcourt Brace Jovanovich, 1980), 3:16.

10. Virginia Woolf, "Rupert Brooke," in *The Essays of Virginia Woolf,* ed. Andrew McNeillie (New York: Harcourt Brace Jovanovich, 1987), 2:280.

11. Virginia Woolf, *The Diary of Virginia Woolf,* ed. Anne Olivier Bell (New York: Harcourt Brace Jovanovich, 1982), 4:235.

12. Jane Emery, *Rose Macaulay: A Writer's Life* (London: John Murray, 1991), 110; hereafter cited in text.

13. Rose Macaulay, *Views and Vagabonds* (London: John Murray, 1912), 57; hereafter cited in text as Macaulay 1912.

14. Rose Macaulay, *Non-Combatants and Others* (1916; London: Methuen, 1986), 121; hereafter cited in text as Macaulay 1916.

15. Brooke was also the principal model for main characters in two unpublished romans à clef written by members of his circle of friends: *Westward Saga* by Reginald Pole and *Novel* by Gwen Raverat. The chief danger for the critic in using any novel allegedly portraying "real" people is, of course, treating it as history and not as fiction. Macaulay's early novels, however, do reveal on many levels what a striking figure Brooke was to his friends.

16. Robert Wohl, *The Generation of 1914* (Cambridge, Mass.: Harvard

University Press, 1979), 89; hereafter cited in text.

17.   Vera Brittain, *Testament of Youth* (1933; N.p.: Wideview Books, 1980), 155.

18.   Quoted in Fred D. Crawford, *British Poets of the Great War* (Selinsgrove: Susquehanna University Press, 1988), 75; hereafter cited in text as Crawford.

19.   Ivor Gurney, *War Letters,* ed. R. K. R. Thornton (London: Hogarth Press, 1984), 29; hereafter cited in text.

20.   Robert Graves, *In Broken Images: Selected Correspondence,* ed. Paul O'Prey (Mt. Kisco, N.Y.: Moyer Bell, 1988), 107; hereafter cited in text.

21.   D. H. Lawrence, *The Selected Letters of D. H. Lawrence,* ed Harry T. Moore (New York: Viking, 1962), 337.

22.   Jonathan Rose, *The Edwardian Temperament: 1895–1919* (Athens. Ohio University Press, 1986), 112, 113.

23.   Paul Fussell, *The Great War and Modern Memory* (London: Oxford University Press, 1977), 24; Rose, 193.

24.   Edmund Blunden, *War Poets 1914–1918,* Writers and Their Work No. 100, The British Council and the National Book League (London: Longmans, Green, 1958), 20; hereafter cited in text.

25.   In editing this volume Larkin had "vaguely supposed" that modern English poetry was "full of good stuff hitherto suppressed by the modernist claque." When he read the works of Brooke's friend Wilfred Gibson, however, he was severely disappointed: "People like this make Rupert Brooke seem colossal." Motion, 362–63.

26.   William York Tindall, *Forces in Modern British Literature* (New York: Vintage, 1956), 307.

27.   B. C. Southam, *A Guide to the "Selected Poems" of T. S. Eliot* (New York: Harcourt Brace Jovanovich, 1968), 72.

28.   Peter Ackroyd, *T. S. Eliot: A Life* (New York: Simon & Schuster, 1984), 20; hereafter cited in text.

29.   Joseph E. Duncan, *The Revival of Metaphysical Poetry* (Minneapolis: University of Minnesota Press, 1959), 120.

30.   T. S. Eliot, *Selected Prose,* ed. Frank Kermode (New York: Harcourt Brace Jovanovich and Farrar, Straus, Giroux, 1975), 41; hereafter cited in text as Eliot 1975.

31.   George Orwell, *Homage to Catalonia* (New York: Harcourt, Brace & World, 1952), 231–32.

Selected Bibliography

PRIMARY SOURCES

The Poetical Works of Rupert Brooke. Edited by Geoffrey Keynes. London: Faber &
Faber, 1946, 1970.
John Webster and the Elizabethan Drama. New York: Russell & Russell, 1916.
Thesis written for fellowship at King's College.
Letters from America. Preface by Henry James. London: Sidgwick & Jackson;
New York: Scribner's, 1916.
Democracy and the Arts. Preface by Geoffrey Keynes. London: Rupert Hart-
Davis, 1946. Essay read to the CUFS on 24 November 1910.
The Prose of Rupert Brooke. Edited by Christopher Hassall. London: Sidgwick &
Jackson, 1956.
The Letters of Rupert Brooke. Edited by Geoffrey Keynes. New York: Harcourt,
Brace & World, 1968.

SECONDARY SOURCES

Bibliographies

Keynes, Geoffrey. *A Bibliography of Rupert Brooke.* London: Rupert Hart-Davis;
Fair Lawn, N.J.: Essential Books, 1954.

Books and Parts of Books

Browne, Maurice. *Recollections of Rupert Brooke.* Chicago: Alexander Green, 1927.
Short yet interesting memoir by a theatrical producer who met Brooke in
Chicago on Brooke's return to England. Browne resists the myth in some
particulars and at other times yields to it, but flashes of the real Brooke
do shine through.
Cheason, Denis. *The Cambridgeshire of Rupert Brooke.* Waterbridge,
Cambridgeshire: Dennis Cheason, 1980. Text of "The Old Vicarage,
Grantchester," along with drawings of and texts about all the place-
names mentioned in the poem.
Conrad, Peter. "Aesthetic America." In *Imagining America.* New York: Oxford
University Press, 1980. Discusses Brooke's *Letters from America,* along
with Oscar Wilde's travels there. Brooke as touring Apostle.
De la Marc, Walter. *Rupert Brooke and the Intellectual Imagination.* London:
Sidgwick & Jackson, 1919. Text of a lecture given at Rugby in March

1919. Surprisingly uninformative, with some curious misperceptions about Brooke's poetry, among them that it lacks "reverie, a deep still broodingness" and that "The instant that love is dead, he has, to put it crudely, very little use for its corpse."

Delaney, Paul. *The Neo-Pagans: Rupert Brooke and the Ordeal of Youth.* New York: Free Press, 1987. Solid use of the Brooke Archives, with some true revelations. Best considered as its title indicates: Brooke in his social scene. The poetry is considered mainly from the purely biographical standpoint.

Drinkwater, John. "Rupert Brooke." In *The Muse in Council.* Boston: Houghton Mifflin, 1925. A furtherance of the personal myth; difficult to believe that Drinkwater actually knew Brooke. Certainly it appears he did not know the real Brooke, or preferred not to discuss it. Better insights on the poetry, from a traditional Georgian perspective.

Hassall, Christopher. *Rupert Brooke.* New York: Harcourt, Brace & World, 1964. The standard biography, and while somewhat overprotective, at least attempts to provide a balanced picture. Heavy reliance on Brooke's letters, because it appeared before Keynes's edition of the *Letters* and because Hassall died before he could correct the proofs. Underdocumented.

Hastings, Michael. *The Handsomest Young Man in England: Rupert Brooke.* London: Michael Joseph, 1967. Taken by some to be an antithesis to Hassall's depiction of Brooke, it is more an overreaction to Hassall's values, and more vehemently to Stringer's, than to the figure of Brooke. Cumbersome misreadings of several poems, as well as their cultural milieu, but some solid insights. Profusely illustrated.

Hynes, Samuel. "Rupert Brooke." In *Edwardian Occasions.* Oxford: Oxford University Press, 1972. Good example of the conventional reaction against Brooke's initial reputation: an anticaricature.

Larkin, Philip. "The Apollo Bit." In *Required Writing: Miscellaneous Pieces 1955–1982,* 177–81. New York: Farrar Straus Giroux, 1984. Review of Keynes's edition of the Letters. Larkin does not see the necessity for omitting portions of the letters, and divides Brooke's life into four sections, of which the last (post-Tahiti) is "the most interesting."

Lehmann, John. *The Strange Destiny of Rupert Brooke.* New York: Holt, Rinehart & Winston, 1981 (published in Great Britain in 1980 as *Rupert Brooke: His Life and His Legend*). The best short work on Brooke, eminently balanced. Some small misgaugings of biographical episodes and social background, and again an overreliance on the letters, but well written with a sane scope.

Marsh, Edward. *Rupert Brooke: A Memoir.* First printed with *Collected Poems.* London: Sidgwick & Jackson, 1918. Generally criticized as perpetuating the blithe Apollo myth of Brooke; its graver fault is an overreliance on a carefully chosen and edited selection of Brooke's letters.

Millard, Kenneth. "Rupert Brooke: 'The Strife of Limbs.'" In *Edwardian Poetry*. Oxford: Clarendon Press, 1991. Solid attempt to "recover" Brooke for what is important in his work, but marred by the thesis that there were no Georgians, only Edwardians and modernists.

Nesbitt, Cathleen. *A Little Love and Good Company*. Owings Mills, Md.: Stemmer House, 1977. Interesting account of Brooke's last major passion.

Pearsall, Robert Brainard. *Rupert Brooke: The Man and Poet*. Amsterdam: Rodopi, 1974. The first work to consult the Brooke Archives at King's, but disappointing: sprinkled with minor errors of fact. Some good observations about Brooke from a psychological viewpoint, but essentially gets the shape of Brooke's life wrong.

Rogers, Timothy. Rupert Brooke: *A Reappraisal and Selection from His Writings, Some Hitherto Unpublished*. New York: Barnes & Noble, 1971. The Best of Brooke volume that Rogers had asked for three years earlier (see later entry). Divides Brooke's career into different facets, each solidly introduced and carefully selected.

Stringer, Arthur. *Red Wine of Youth*. Indianapolis: Bobbs-Merrill, 1948. Probably no other literary figure has inspired so much bad writing as Brooke, and this biography is the worst example. Based on materials collected by adventurer-writer Richard Halliburton, and turgidly overwritten to the point of unreadablity, it perpetuates the "sunny Apollo" myth, while providing a few interesting facts.

Articles

Fromm, Gloria. "Saving Rupert Brooke." *New Criterion* 6 (September 1987): 71–77. Review of Delaney's *Neo-Pagans*, finding that Brooke is not merely dead but "obsolete."

Levenback, Karen L. "Virginia Woolf and Rupert Brooke: Poised Between Olympus and the 'Real World.'" *Virginia Woolf Miscellany* 33 (Fall 1989): 5–6. Shows that Brooke was sympathetic to Woolf during one of her breakdowns (they were treated by the same doctor), and surmises that Woolf to some degree repressed knowledge of Brooke's death.

Moeyes, Paul. "Georgian Poetry's False Dawn (A Reassessment of Rupert Brooke: His Poetry and Personality." *Neophilologus* 75 (July 1991): 456–69. Claims that Brooke was essentially an unoriginal chameleon, that every stage of his life—decadent, Fabian, neopagan—was a pose, and that the war sonnets are the product of his last pose, that of a high-society "Soul." Declares Brooke is "a transitional figure" to writers of the 1920s such as F. Scott Fitzgerald and Evelyn Waugh.

Read, Alan Walker. "Onomastic Devices in the Poetry of Rupert Brooke." *Literary Onomastic Studies* 9 (1982): 183–208. A listing of the uses Brooke made of names in his poetry, but with little analysis.

Rogers, Timothy. "Rupert Brooke: Man and Monument." *English* 17 (Autumn
    1968): 79–84. Review of Keynes's edition of the Letters, with solid criti-
    cism of Hastings's book, by a would-be biographer. Last paragraph,
    which calls for *The Best of Brooke,* lays out the rationale for Rogers's own
    book on Brooke.
Thomas, W. K. "The War Sonnets of Rupert Brooke." *English Quarterly* 7
    (Spring 1974): 27–53. Excellent analysis of the way the sonnets relate to
    each other, and in the context of English literary history; only slightly
    weaker on placing them in the context of Brooke's life.

Index

The Author

William E. Laskowski is an associate professor of English at Jamestown College and has taught English and writing at the University of Illinois at Chicago, Chicago State University, Bradley University, and Jamestown College. He has written about Richard Wagner and M. R. James and has published a bibliography of the works of Leon Edel and articles about science fiction and the place of George Orwell in English radical tradition.